NEW MATHS FRAMEWORKING

Functional Skills

Keith Gordon, Chris Pearce, Trevor Senior

William Collins' dream of knowledge for all began with the publication of his first book in 1819. A self-educated mill worker, he not only enriched millions of lives, but also founded a flourishing publishing house. Today, staying true to this spirit, Collins books are packed with inspiration, innovation and practical expertise. They place you at the centre of a world of possibility and give you exactly what you need to explore it.

Collins. Do more.

Published by Collins
An imprint of HarperCollins*Publishers*
77 – 85 Fulham Palace Road
Hammersmith
London
W6 8JB

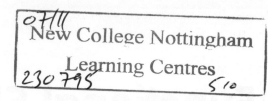

Browse the complete Collins catalogue at
www.collinseducation.com

10 9 8 7 6 5 4

ISBN-13 978 0 00 731844 5

Keith Gordon, Chris Pearce and Trevor Senior assert their moral rights to be identified as the authors of this work

Project managed by Letitia Luff
Edited and proofread by Joan Miller
Cover design, content design and typesetting by Linda Miles, Lodestone Publishing Limited
Illustrations by Jerry Fowler
Production by Therese Webb

Printed and bound by Martins the Printers, Berwick-upon-Tweed

British Library Cataloguing in Publication Data
A Catalogue record for this publication is available from the British Library

This book is proudly printed on paper which contains wood from well managed forests, certified in accordance with the rules of the Forest Stewardship Council. For more information about FSC, please visit www.fsc-uk.org

Mixed Sources
Product group from well-managed forests and other controlled sources
www.fsc.org Cert no. SW-COC-1806
© 1996 Forest Stewardship Council
FSC

Contents

Activities

⭐ Beginner

⭐⭐ Improver

⭐⭐⭐ Advanced

Rich Tasks

Introduction

This is not a mathematics text book.

This book is not about teaching you any new mathematical techniques and tricks. You know lots already.

What this book is about

- Showing you that mathematics can be used to help tackle real-life problems.
- Helping to improve your confidence in using mathematics.
- Encouraging you to apply the mathematical skills you have in new situations.
- Developing your ability to interpret results and decide how successful you have been.
- Giving you the chance to work with others and talk about mathematics.

What you will get out of it

- The chance to use the mathematical skills you have in a realistic context.
- Opportunities to work with others.
- An understanding of why mathematics can be useful in life and work.
- Greater confidence about your own ability to use mathematics.
- Interesting and enjoyable mathematics lessons.

Some things to think about

- People who can use mathematics confidently get the most out of life learning and work. That could be you.
- Do not worry about making mistakes. A lot of the tasks in this book have more than one right answer. We want to know **your** solution and we want you to be able to explain how you obtained it.
- Mathematics can be interesting, useful and exciting. We hope to convince you that this is true.

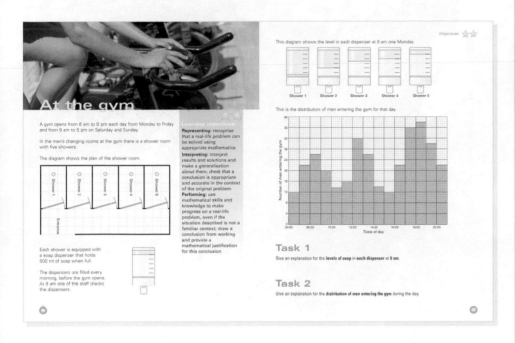

Star ratings
See how much an activity will challenge you. One star means you are just starting to explore Functional Skills, three stars and you are well on your way to mastering them.

Learning objectives
Understand the skills you will be practising in the activity. Check to see how many you feel confident using from the list on the back page of this book.

Setting the scene
Find out about the context in which the activity is set by looking at the photographs and reading the introduction. Some will be familiar, some you may never have heard of!

Activities
Flex your functional muscles with a range of exercises, questions and tasks. You will need to approach them in different ways so remember to read what you are being asked to do carefully.

Extension tasks
Think that you are fully functional? Stretch yourself by taking it a step further.

Activities

Endangered species

An endangered species is any species that is considered to be in danger of extinction. There are over 100 different animal species that are classed as endangered.

The table on the next page gives some data about a few endangered species. Use the information to answer the following questions, then move onto the tasks.

The table on the next page gives some data about a few endangered species.

Warm-up questions

1   What is the **average normal lifespan** of a **whale**?

2   Do animals generally have **shorter or longer** lives in **captivity** than in the **wild**?

3   Approximately **how many lions** existed in Africa in **1950**?

4   Are **male chimpanzees** generally **heavier** or **lighter** than **female chimpanzees**?

5   You are told that a **grizzly bear** weighs **700 lbs**. Do you think it is **male or female**?

Learning objectives

Representing: decide how to represent the problem to make it easier to solve using mathematics

Analysing: use appropriate mathematical procedures

Interpreting: interpret results and solutions and make a generalisation about them

Performing: use a range of mathematics to find solutions

Links with
ICT, Science, Geography

Animal	Population	Size	Lifespan
Bat	Some bat populations are counted in millions. Others are extremely low or declining.	Large bats can have a wingspan of 6 feet. Small bats can be less than an inch long.	Most bats live longer than most mammals of the same size. The longest known lifespan of a bat in the wild is about 30–40 years.
Grizzly bear	In 1950 there were about 50 000 grizzly bears in North America. Now there are about 1000 remaining, in five separate populations. In Alaska, there are over 30 000 grizzly bears.	**Height:** about $3-3\frac{1}{2}$ feet at shoulders **Length:** 6–7 feet **Adult weight:** male 300–850 lbs; female 200–450 lbs	20–25 years
Whale	Varies with each species.	**Length:** varies, up to 110 feet **Weight:** varies, up to 150 tons	Whales normally live 20–40 years but they can live up to 80 years.
Lion	The lion population in Africa has reduced by half since the early 1950s. Today, fewer than 21 000 remain in all of Africa.	**Height:** males reach 4 feet, females are smaller **Length:** males reach 5-8 feet, females are smaller **Weight:** males reach 330–500 lbs, females weigh less	13 years, although they may live longer in captivity
Chimpanzee	An estimated 100 000 to 200 000 chimpanzees live in the wild.	**Height:** approximately 4 feet **Weight:** males 90–120 lbs, females 60–110 lbs	Chimpanzees rarely live past the age of 50 in the wild, but have been known to reach the age of 60 in captivity.

Task 1

Using the different **column headings**, sort the animals into any **order** that you think is appropriate. When you have **insufficient information**, you will need to make **decisions**. Consider whether there is a **link** between the **population** and **lifespan** of these animals.

Task 2

Prepare a **15-minute presentation** about **endangered species** for your mathematics class. Include **mathematical facts**. Use books or the internet to **research other endangered species** and then **present your findings**.

Task 3

You may need to use the **information** given in the **table** at the start of this activity to answer these questions.

1   What is the **maximum length** of a **whale**, in **metres**?

> 1 foot = 30 centimetres

2   A **lion** weighs **400 lbs**.

    How many **kilograms** does this lion weigh?

> 1 kg ≈ 2.2 lb

3   Work out the number of **grizzly bears** remaining altogether in the **five separate populations**, as a **percentage** of the **number in the US** in 1950.

4   **Bats** are the **slowest** mammals on Earth to reproduce. At **birth**, a **pup** weighs up to **25%** of its **mother's body weight**. If a **mother bat** weighs **8 grams**, how much could the **pup** weigh?

5   Before the current levels of whaling, the **humpback whale population** was **150 000**. The population has since **fallen** to **one-sixth** of this value. What is the **population now**?

6   The **DNA** of **chimpanzees** and **humans** are about **98.4% similar**. What percentage is not similar?

Football

This activity is based on the English football league.

Task 1

There are 20 teams in the **English Premiership**. In a season, every team plays every other team twice, once at their ground (**home**) and once at the other team's ground (**away**). This means that, in a season, each team plays 38 matches.

If the team **wins** they get **3 points**. If they **draw** they get **1 point**. If they **lose** they get **no points**. If two teams have the same number of points then the team with the bigger **goal difference** will be higher placed.

> **Goal difference** is simply the number of goals scored **for** the team **minus** the number of goals scored **against** the team.

Learning objectives

Representing: decide how to represent the problem to make it easier to solve using mathematics

Analysing: establish a pattern or relationship and then change the variables to see how this changes the results

Interpreting: test generalisations and draw conclusions from the mathematical analysis

Performing: analyse the situation or problem and decide which is the appropriate mathematical method needed to tackle it

Links with ICT and PE

1   How many **matches** are played altogether in a **Premier league season**?

2   A team has **scored 48 goals** and has **12 goals scored against it**. What is their goal difference?

3   A team has **scored 15 goals** and has a **goal difference of −8**. How many goals have been scored against the team?

4   Explain why, if the **goal differences for all 20 teams** are added up, the total will be **zero**.

5   If **after 10 games** a team has **won 4 matches**, **drawn 3** and **lost 3**, how many **points** would they have?

6 What is the **maximum number of points** that a team could possibly have **at the end of a season**?

7 In the 2003–2004 season Arsenal went all season without losing a match.

  a What was the **minimum number of points** they could have had?

  b In fact they had 90 points. Work out the **combinations of wins and draws** that would give this number of points **over 38 matches**.

8 In the 2004–5 season Chelsea **won the league with 95 points**. They **won 29 games**. How many games did they draw and how many did they lose?

9 At the end of the 2007–8 season the **bottom club**, Derby County, had **11 points**. There are **four ways** to obtain this number of points. What are the **four combinations of wins, losses and draws**?

10 This scattergram shows the **points** and **goal differences** for all 20 teams in the premiership at the end of the 2007–8 season.

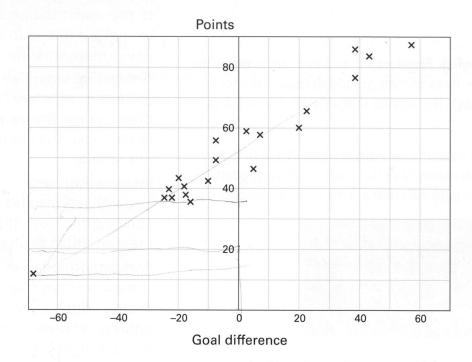

Read each of these statements and write down whether it is true or false.

  a The teams with the **most points** had the **greatest goal difference**.

  b There must always be the **same number of teams** with a **positive goal difference** as there are with a **negative goal difference**.

  c The top team scored **over 100 goals** more than the bottom team.

  d If a team had had a **points total of 20** they would probably have had a **goal difference of about –40**.

Task 2

The FA Cup is a knock-out competition. It has been played every year since 1871, except for during the two world wars. Clubs in the senior leagues around the country and all of the teams in the Premiership, Championship and Leagues 1 and 2 are entitled to enter.

There are preliminary rounds and the competition proper consists of **8 rounds**, with the final being played at Wembley. In the 2008–9 season 762 teams were accepted into the competition. The first qualifying round was held on 16 August 2008. The first proper round was held on 8 November and the final was held on 30 May between Manchester United and Everton.

1   Two teams compete in the **final**, which is **round 8** of the competition proper. In **round 7** (the semi-finals), there were **4 teams** competing. In **round 6** (the quarter-finals), there were **8 teams** competing. How many teams competed in the first round proper?

2   In 2008–9, how many teams had been **eliminated** before the proper competition started?

3   In a cup competition with **10 rounds**, how many teams would be in the **first round**?

4   For a cup competition with *n* rounds, write down a rule for the number of teams that would be in the first round.

Task 3

> **The final score in a match is 3–2.**
>
> **How many possible half-time scores are there?**

Investigate this and come up with **a rule** for the number of possible half-time scores for any given final score.

1   Decide how to represent the problem, for example, in a diagram or a table, to make it easier to use mathematics to solve it.

2   Establish a pattern or relationship and then change the variables to see how this changes the results.

3   Test your generalisations and draw conclusions from the mathematical analysis.

4   Analyse the situation or problem and decide which is the most appropriate mathematical method that you would use to tackle it.

Paving

In this activity, suppose you are a builder. A customer has asked you to lay paving slabs to cover an area of her garden. You need to draw up the plans.

Garden: 60 metres x 10 metres
1 metre = 100 cm

60 m

10 m

Prices

- Square slabs cost £12 each or £99 for a pack of 10.

- Rectangular slabs cost £18 each or £120 for a pack of 10.

- Triangular slabs cost £6 each or £49 for a pack of 10.

20 cm
20 cm

30 cm
20 cm

20 cm

Warm-up questions

Use the data above to answer these questions.

1 How many centimetres are in a metre?

2 Four rectangular slabs are put in a line to make a path as shown.

   How long is the path?

3 How much does it cost to buy 25 square slabs? Use the cheapest method.

Learning objectives

Representing: recognise that a real-life problem can be solved using appropriate mathematics; decide how to represent the problem to make it easier to solve using mathematics

Analysing: analyse a pattern or a relationship, using appropriate techniques

Interpreting: interpret results and solutions and make a generalisation about them; check that a conclusion is appropriate and accurate in the context of the original problem

Performing: check work and methods when tackling a problem and decide if a different approach may be more effective; give a solution to a practical problem, even if it is not within a familiar context, and make sure the solution is presented in a clear and understandable way

4 How much does it cost to buy 25 square slabs and 31 rectangular slabs?
Use the cheapest method.

5 What is the area of the garden to be paved, shown in the diagram? State the units in your answer.

6 How much more would it cost to buy 10 single triangular slabs than a pack of 10?

7 How many square slabs would fit in a square metre?

8 How many triangular slabs would cover the same area as 5 square slabs?

9 How many rectangular slabs could you buy for £100?

10 You have £540 to spend. Work out how many square, rectangular and triangular slabs you could buy if you buy the same number of each.

Task 1

Work out how many of the rectangular slabs would be needed to pave the whole garden shown in the diagram.

Task 2

Now design a pattern of slabs to cover an area of the garden, using the square and rectangular slabs.

Task 3

Work out the cost of your design for Task 2.

Task 4

Triangular slabs and square slabs can be fitted together as shown.
Design a pattern, using triangular and square slabs.
Use squared paper or graph paper.

Task 5 (extension)

Either design your own garden or design an L-shaped garden.
Use squared paper or graph paper.
Decide on the dimensions of your garden.
Remember to work out the cost of the slabs for your garden.
You may decide to add extra features to your design.

Money matters 1: Pay

Most people with a job get paid either a wage or a salary.

Most unskilled and semi-skilled workers, such as people who work in factories, stores or offices, are paid weekly by the hour and are known as wage-earners.

Most professionals, such as lawyers, doctors or teachers, are paid by the month and are known as salaried workers.

Wage-earners

There is no maximum for the amount a worker can earn an hour but there is a legally enforced national minimum wage.

There are three levels of minimum wage, and the rates from 1 October 2008 are:

- £5.73 per hour for workers aged 22 years and over
- a development rate of £4.77 per hour for workers aged 18–21 inclusive
- £3.53 per hour for all workers under the age of 18, who are no longer of compulsory school age.

Students at school who do a paper round, for example, can be paid below £3.53 per hour.

Task 1

Copy and complete the table for these workers.

NB: MW means they are paid minimum wage.

Name	Age	Hours	Wage per hour	Total weekly wages
Aftab	30	35	£7.20	
Betty	25	40	MW	
Colin	42	38	£13.50	
Diedre	17	30	MW	
Eddy	28		£8.75	£306.25
Frank	21		MW	£190.80
Gus	15	8		£22.00
Hinna	25	37.5		£367.50
Ian		36	MW	£171.72
Jemima		20	MW	£70.60

Overtime

Most wage-earners have a **fixed number of hours** that they have to work each week, typically around 40 hours. If they are required to work beyond these hours then they will get paid **overtime**. The pay rate for overtime will be **more than** the normal rate. For example, overtime may be paid at **time-and-a-half**, which means that a worker normally earning £8 per hour would get £12 per hour for overtime paid at time-and-a-half.

Task 2

Copy and complete this table.

NB: MW means they are paid minimum wage.

Name	Age	Basic hours	Overtime hours	Basic wage per hour	Overtime rate	Total wages
Alf	32	35	10	£8.20	1.5 x	
Belinda	27	40	6	MW	1.25 x	
Chas	42	36	8	£11.50	1.5 x	
Dave	17	35	5	MW	2 x	
Edith	29	40		£8.75	1.4 x	£411.25
Francis	20	35		MW	1.5 x	£195.57
Gaynor	14	10	2		1.5 x	£41.60
Henry	26	40	6		1.25 x	£427.50
Iris		38	8	MW	1.5 x	£238.50
Jack		35	10	MW	1.25 x	£167.68

Salaried staff

Workers who are paid a **salary** get the **same pay each month**, even though some months are shorter than others. This is calculated by **dividing the annual salary by 12**.

Salaried workers do not usually work overtime, although they may have a **fixed number of hours**. If they work beyond the required number of hours they may be allowed a **day off to compensate** or **receive a bonus payment**.

Task 3

Copy and complete this table.

Name	Monthly salary	Annual salary
Pete	£2500	
Quinlan	£3350	
Rosie		£22 500
Sue		£74 520
Teresa	£4180	

Extension questions

1   Arnold works a basic **35-hour week** for a basic wage of **£9.50 per hour**. One week he works his basic hours plus **8 hours'** overtime at **time-and-a-half** and another **8 hours'** overtime at **double time**. What is Arnold's **total wage**?

2   Bettina, 20, who is on **minimum wage**, works a basic week of **40 hours** from Monday to Friday. She does an **extra hour each day** from **Monday to Friday** at **time-and-a-quarter** and then works **8 hours** on Sunday for **time-and-a-half**. What is Bettina's **total wage** for that week?

3   Colleen works a basic week of **38 hours**. She also works **6 hours'** overtime at **time-and-a-half** and **4 hours'** overtime at **double time**. Her **total wage** for that week is **£412.50**. What is Colleen's **hourly rate**?

4   Derek is paid **minimum wage** and works a basic week of **40 hours**. He also does **6 hours'** overtime at **time-and-a-quarter** and the **same number of hours'** overtime at **time-and-a-half**. His total wage is **£269.51**. How **old** is Derek?

5   Erica works **8 hours** each day from Monday to Friday. She is paid **minimum wage**. **Wednesday** last week was her **22nd birthday**. What was her **total wage** for that week?

Wales

In this activity, you will find out about more about Wales, which is an important part of the UK. You will need to refer to the Data sheet: Wales.

Task 1

Use the information given on the Data sheet: Wales to answer these questions.

1 What **percentage** of **people living in Wales in 1981** were **born** in Wales?

2 In what **year** could **half** of the people living in Wales **speak Welsh**?

3 How many **miles** of **coastline** are there in **Wales**? Give your answer to the **nearest 10 miles**.

4 What is the **height of Snowdon**, to the **nearest 100 feet**?

5 In **April 2001**, which **age group** had the **greatest proportion** of people able to **speak, read and write Welsh**?

6 There are **40 Welsh MPs**. How many are **women**?

7 Work out the difference between the **highest and lowest** recorded **temperatures** in Wales.

8 In **what year** did the proportion of people **able to speak Welsh** start to **increase**?

9 Work out the **area** of Wales that is **either National Park or an Area of outstanding natural beauty**.

10 How many people **living in Wales** are aged **under 16**?

Task 2

The **village** with the **longest name** in Wales is in Anglesey and is

LLANFAIRPWLLGWYNGYLLGOGERYCHWYNDROBWYLLLLANTYSILIOGOGOGOCH

It has **58 letters**, or **51 in the Welsh alphabet**, in which ch and ll count as single letters.

1   Using the **English alphabet**, complete the tally chart for the letters **A, G, L, O, W, Y** and **others**.

Letter	Tally	Frequency
A		
G		
L		
O		
W		
Y		
Others		

2   Using centimetre-squared paper, draw a **bar chart** to represent the information from question 1.

3   Now use your results to answer these questions.
   a   Which letter is the **mode**?
   b   **One letter** is chosen **at random** from the name. What is the **probability** that it is the letter **G**?
   c   **One letter** is chosen **at random** from the name. What is the **probability** that it is **not** the letter **G**?

Task 3

Here is a **map** of Wales.

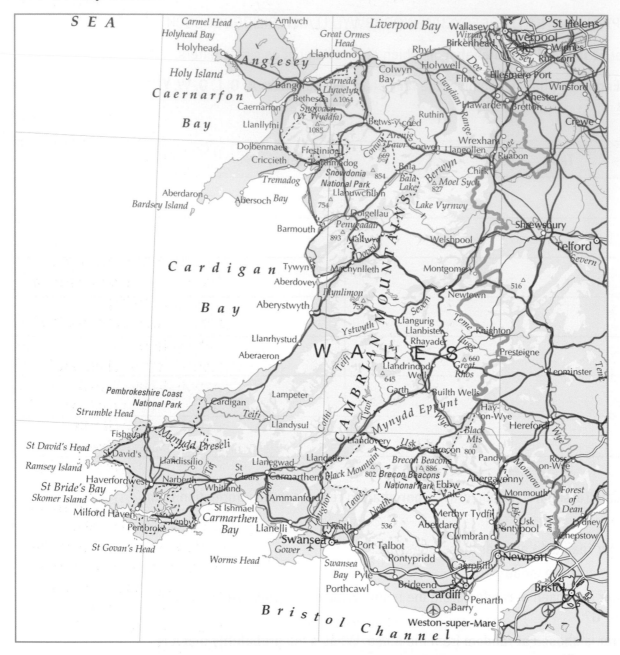

Complete the sentences **as accurately as possible**, using one of the following **directions**.

> north   east   south   west   north-east   north-west   south-east   south-west

1 **Cardiff** is … of **Swansea**.

2 **Tywyn** is … of **Aberystwyth**.

3 **Cardigan** is … of **Fishguard**.

4 **Bangor** is … of **Holyhead**.

5 **Swansea** is … of **Brecon**.

6 **Holyhead** is … of **Colwyn Bay**.

Bricklaying patterns

This is a typical house brick.

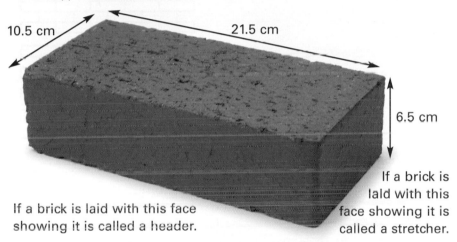

10.5 cm

21.5 cm

6.5 cm

If a brick is laid with this face showing it is called a header.

If a brick is laid with this face showing it is called a stretcher.

When bricks are used to build walls they need to be laid so that they are strong enough to support floors and roofs. Bricks laid in an interesting pattern can also add to the visual attractiveness of a property.

There are many different arrangements of bricks. For example, one of the most common is the arrangement below, left, which is called Stretcher bond. The arrangement below, right, is called Flemish bond and is made with alternating stretchers (the bricks that lie along the wall) and headers (the bricks that lie across the wall). It is a very strong arrangement and is used when a wall is two bricks thick.

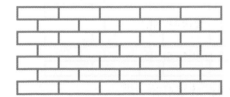

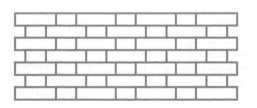

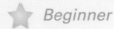
Imagine that these brick patterns continue in all directions. What are the symmetries?

The Stretcher bond has the following symmetries:

- a vertical line of symmetry through the centre of any brick

- a horizontal line of symmetry through the centre of any brick

- rotational symmetry of order 2 through the centre of any brick or the centre of any vertical join.

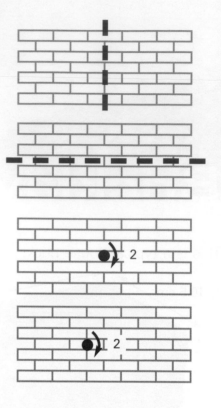

Task 1

Describe the **symmetries** to be found in the **Flemish bond** pattern.

Task 2

Describe the **symmetries** to be found in **each** of the following brick patterns.

Stack bond

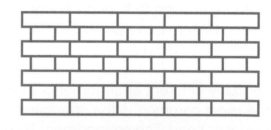

English bond

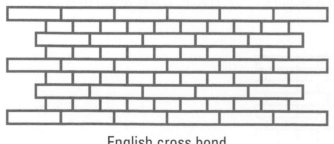

English cross bond

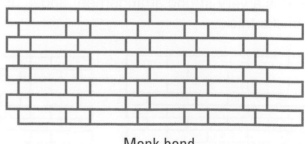

Monk bond

Task 3

Bricks are also used in **pavements** and are laid in various patterns.

Four **paving patterns** are shown below. Describe the **symmetries** of each one.

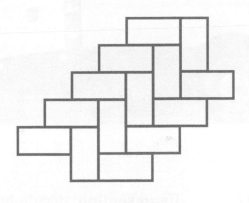

Herringbone

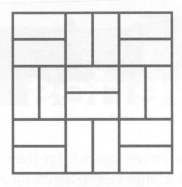

Basketweave

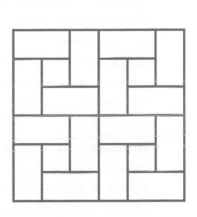

Pinwheel

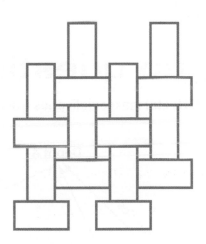

De laRobia weave

Deliveries

Courier companies deliver parcels for their customers. They usually have several large warehouses throughout the country. The parcels are sent to these warehouses, then sent out to smaller depots for local delivery. It is important for the warehouse manager to plan routes that are as short as possible, but that cover all the depots.

Warm-up questions

On-time couriers (OTC Ltd) makes deliveries from its warehouse to three local depots.

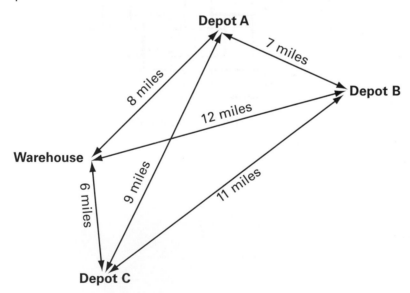

1   How far does a van travel if it goes from the **warehouse** to **depot A** and then to **depot C** and back to the **warehouse**?

2   If the van travels at **30 mph** how long does it take to travel **from the warehouse to depot B**?

Learning objectives

Representing: decide how to show the initial problem, using mathematical symbols; decide which methods to use to make progress with the solution

Analysing: analyse a pattern or a relationship using appropriate techniques

Interpreting: interpret results and solutions and make a generalisation about them; check that a conclusion is appropriate and accurate in the context of the original problem

Performing: use a range of mathematics to find solutions

3   If a van can carry **35 parcels**, how many journeys would be needed to take
     200 parcels?

4   How much does it cost for a van to travel **150 miles** at **80p** per mile?

5   How much does it cost for a van to travel **150 miles** every day for **1 working week**
     (6 days)?

Task 1

As warehouse manager for OTC Ltd, refer back to the plan and work out the **shortest route**
for a driver who must visit **all three depots** and **return to the warehouse**.

Task 2

The company opens a new depot called **depot D**.

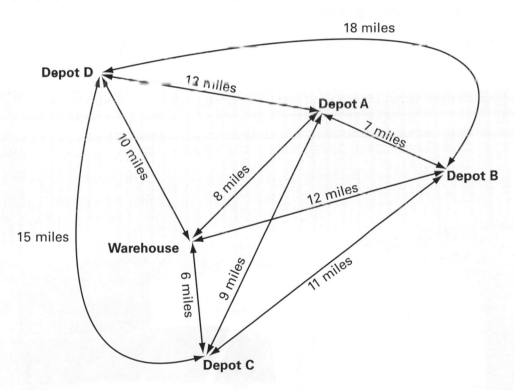

Work out the **shortest route** for a driver who must visit **all four depots** and **return to the
warehouse**.

Task 3

The company decides to use **two delivery vans**.

Work out the best way that they could **share deliveries** to **all four depots** and **return to the warehouse**.

The **running costs per mile** for each van is **80p**.

Compare the **daily costs** for using **one and two vans**.

State any **advantages** or **disadvantages** of using one or two vans.
State clearly any **assumptions** you make.

Task 4

A delivery company has its warehouse in **Sheffield**.

Deliveries are made to depots in **Nottingham**, **Leeds**, **York** and **Huddersfield**.

Use the **internet** to work out a **mileage chart** or **diagram**.

Decide the best routes, if the company has one or two vans that return to the warehouse.

Water

Each person in Britain uses an average of about 150 litres (33 gallons) of water per day.

The pie chart gives a breakdown of how that water is used.

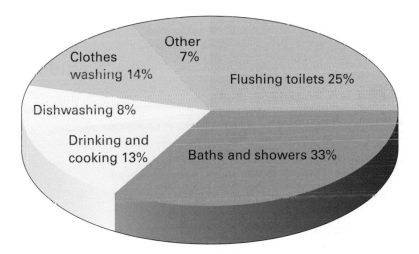

Pie chart labels:
- Other 7%
- Clothes washing 14%
- Flushing toilets 25%
- Dishwashing 8%
- Drinking and cooking 13%
- Baths and showers 33%

All households pay for the water they use each year.

On the next page is a typical bill. The labels describe what each item on it means.

This bill is for a three-bedroom bungalow, occupied by a couple and their teenage son. There are two bathrooms, each with a toilet and shower.

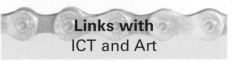

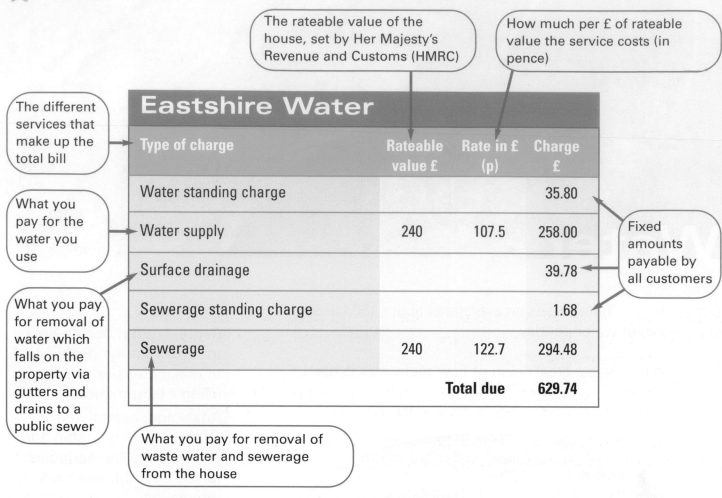

The rateable value of the house, set by Her Majesty's Revenue and Customs (HMRC)

How much per £ of rateable value the service costs (in pence)

The different services that make up the total bill

What you pay for the water you use

What you pay for removal of water which falls on the property via gutters and drains to a public sewer

What you pay for removal of waste water and sewerage from the house

Fixed amounts payable by all customers

Eastshire Water

Type of charge	Rateable value £	Rate in £ (p)	Charge £
Water standing charge			35.80
Water supply	240	107.5	258.00
Surface drainage			39.78
Sewerage standing charge			1.68
Sewerage	240	122.7	294.48
		Total due	629.74

Task 1

1 Work out how many **litres** of water **per day** each of the items in the pie chart would be for an **average person**. Give your answers to the **nearest litre**.

2 Approximately how many **litres** are there in a **gallon**?

Task 2

A typical **house brick** is **21.5 cm** by **10.25 cm** by **6.5 cm**. It is recommended that, to save water, households place a house brick **in the toilet cistern**.

A litre is **1000 cm³**. A toilet cistern holds about **6 litres** of water. An average person flushes a toilet about **6 times** a day.

Work out approximately how much water is saved **in a year** by adding a house brick to the toilet cistern.

Task 3

1 A house has a **rateable value of £200**. Work out their **annual bill** for water if they get their water from Eastshire Water.

2 A house has a **rateable vale of £175**. Work out their **annual bill** for water if they get their water from Eastshire Water.

3 The householder whose bill has already been studied changes water suppliers to Westshire Water. Their rate for **water supply** is **99.3p** and for **sewerage** is **115.4p**. Their **standing charges** are the same as Eastshire Water. Work out how much **less** their bill will be with Westshire Water.

Task 4

Water meters are usually fitted free by water companies but can cost up to £200 to fit. The water used is charged at about **0.3p per litre**, which includes **water supply and sewerage**. **Standing charges** and **surface drainage** still apply.

1 Assuming that the **3 people** in the bungalow use the **average amount of water** each day, work out how much they would pay **annually** if they had a water meter fitted.

2 If the **installation** of the meter cost **£200**, approximately **how many years** would it be before the **savings** covered the cost of the meter?

Task 5

This is part of a newspaper article.

1 Approximately how many **litres** of water are used in a **bathtub**?

2 A person drinks **4 cups** of coffee a **day**. Approximately how many **bathtubs** of water each **year** will be used to produce the ingredients for the coffee this person drinks?

Shocking but true! If you are a stickler for environmental issues, even you might be surprised at the amount of water you use! A recent British report has suggested that the average person in the UK uses 4500 litres of water daily – that it is roughly about 58 bathtubs full of water every day.

A report estimated that while each person in the UK uses around 150 litres of mains water every day, they consume about 30 times as much in 'virtual' water embedded in food, clothes and other items.

For example, just one tomato from Morocco takes 13 litres of water to grow while the ingredients in a cup of coffee collectively use 140 litres. A shirt made from cotton grown in Pakistan or Uzbekistan soaks up 2700 litres of water.

Task 6 (extension)

Produce a poster or a slide show to show water usage and how we can all conserve water by following a few simple rules.

Pilots of aircraft have to operate according to air law, in the same way that drivers of vehicles have to obey the *Highway Code*.

Flight levels

Aircraft flying quite high use flight levels (FLs) to describe the altitude of the aircraft.

When air traffic controllers and pilots transmit or write down flight levels they leave out the last two zeros of the altimeter reading.

> **FL 50** (flight level five zero) means an altitude of **5000 feet**.
> **FL 45** (flight level four five) means an altitude of **4500 feet**.
> **FL 150** (flight level one five zero) means an altitude of **15 000 feet**.
> Flight levels are only used for **intervals of 500 feet** up to **FL 250** (25 000 feet) and then only **every 1000 feet** above **FL 250**.
> For example, FL 35, FL40, FL45, up to FL 250, then FL 260, FL270 and so on.

Safety in the UK

The semi-circular rule

For safety reasons, aircraft flying in different directions need to fly at different heights.

Aircraft flying in controlled airspace in the UK must fly at a cruising flight level according to the semi-circular rule, as shown in this table and in the diagram that follow.

Learning objectives

Representing: recognise that a real-life problem can be solved using appropriate mathematics

Analysing: analyse a pattern or a relationship using appropriate techniques

Interpreting: give a conclusion or answer to the original problem, using language and forms of presentation that make sense to a wider population

Performing: give a solution to a practical problem, even if it is not within a familiar context, and make sure the solution is presented in a clear and understandable way; draw a conclusion from working and provide a mathematical justification for this conclusion

Links with
ICT

(Magnetic track) 000° to 179°	(Magnetic track) 180° to 359°
FL 10	FL 20
FL 30	FL 40
FL 50	FL 60
FL 70	FL 80
FL 90	FL 100
FL 110	FL 120
FL 130	FL 140
FL 150	FL 160
Up to FL 410, then every 4000 feet	Up to FL 400, then every 4000 feet

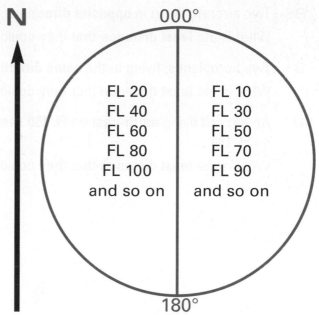

Questions

Use the information given above to answer these questions.

1 What is **6500 feet**, written as a **flight level**?

2 What is **FL 280** written in **feet**?

3 Explain why **FL 34** is not used.

4 An aircraft is flying on a **bearing of 070°**.
Using the **semi-circular rule**, at which of these **flight levels** could it fly?
FL 100   FL 110   FL 120   FL 130

5 An aircraft is flying on a **bearing of 290°**.
Using the **semi-circular rule**, at which of these **flight levels** could it fly?
FL 100   FL 110   FL 120   FL 130

6 An aircraft is flying **westwards**.
Using the **semi-circular rule**, at which of these **flight levels** could it fly?
FL 100   FL 110   FL 120   FL 130

7 An aircraft is flying **eastwards**.
Using the **semi-circular rule**, at which of these **flight levels** could it fly?
FL 100   FL 110   FL 120   FL 130

8   Two aircraft, flying in **opposite directions**, are using the **semi-circular rule**.
    What is the **least distance** that they could be **apart**?

9   Two aeroplanes, flying in the **same direction**, are using the **semi-circular rule**.
    What is the **least distance** that they could be **apart**?

10 An aircraft flying **north-east** on **FL 150** sees another aircraft flying **south-east**
    on **FL 190**.
    What is the **least distance** that they could be **apart**?

Darts

Darts is a popular game. Players take it in turns to throw three darts at a board like the one shown here.

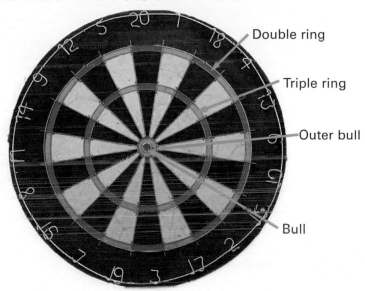

Double ring

Triple ring

Outer bull

Bull

Depending where the dart lands, it can score any number, from the lowest score of 1 to the highest possible score of 60.

There are 20 sectors. Each sector is worth the score shown on the outside.

Around the outside of each sector is the double ring. If a dart lands in this ring it scores double the value of the sector. Halfway in there is another, smaller ring called the triple ring. A dart landing in this ring scores treble the value of the sector.

In the very centre is a small circle surrounded by a small ring. The middle circle is called the bull and scores 50. The small ring is called the outer bull and scores 25.

The most common darts game is 501. Players take it in turn to throw their darts and their total score is deducted from 501. The first player to finish, by reducing the score to 0, wins. However, to finish, the last dart to reduce the score to 0 (or to achieve the total of 501) must be a double. The bull counts as a double.

If the final three darts give a total that is greater than the number needed to finish, which means the total scored would be over 501, these throws are void.

Professional darts players are experts at working out finishes for various scores. For example:

- 164 would require treble 20, treble 18 and the bull
- 105 could be treble 15, single 20 and double 20 or treble 19, single 18 and double 15.

Some scores, such as 164, only have one three-dart finish, whereas others, such as 105, have many different three-dart finishes.

Questions

In these questions, **T** means a **treble score**, **D** means a **double score** and **S** means a **single score**.

1   What are the following **totals** for **three darts**?

    a T18, D6, S3   **b** T17, D16, S8

    c D17, S17, S3   **d** T15, D10, D6

    e T19, S18, D4

2   A score of **100** has many **three-dart finishes**. Find a **three-dart finish for 100** in which the **final dart** is:

    a D20   **b** bull   **c** D16.

3   **a** What is the **largest** number that **can** be scored with **three darts**?

    b What is the **smallest** number that **cannot** be scored with **one dart**?

4   All the numbers up to **98** can be scored with a **two-dart finish**. Show a **two-dart finish** for **each** of these numbers.

    a 75   **b** 98   **c** 3

5   Show that **99** is the smallest score that needs a **three-dart** rather than a two-dart **finish**.

6   Assuming the dart hits the board, the **smallest number** that can be scored with **one dart** is **1** and the **largest** is **60** (T20). Work out which scores **between 1 and 60 cannot** be scored with **one dart**.

7   Look at the dartboard on the right.
    The numbers **20 and 3** are on **opposite sectors**. Adding these gives a total of 23.
    Which numbers on **opposite sectors**, when added, give a **total that is**:

    a   a total of 24 (there are 2 answers)

    b   a square number

    c   the smallest total?

8   Look at the dartboard again.
    The numbers **20 and 3** are on **opposite sectors**. Subtracting the **smaller** from the **bigger** gives a **difference of 17**.
    Which numbers on **opposite sectors** have a **difference that is**:

    a   12 (there are 2 answers)

    b   a square number

    c   the biggest possible?

9   Look at the dartboard again.
    The numbers **20** and **5** are on **adjacent sectors**. Adding these gives a **total of 25**.
    Which numbers on **adjacent sectors**, when added, give a **total that is**:

    a   25 (there are 2 more answers)

    b   a square number other than 25

    c   19 (there are 4 answers)

    d   the largest possible?

10   The **total** of **all the numbers** on the dartboard is:

     $1 + 2 + 3 + 4 + 5 + 6 + 7 + 8 + 9 + 10 + 11 + 12 + 13 + 14 + 15 + 16 + 17 + 18 + 19 + 20$

     The answer is **210**. Explain an **easy way** to work this out **without adding up all the numbers**.

     Hint: 10 + 11 = 21 and 9 + 12 = 21.

Extension question

The lowest possible number of darts that can be thrown to score **501** and **finish on a double** is **9**.

Work out **how this can be done**. There is more than one answer.

Bridges

In this activity, you will find out about the Humber bridge, then you will design and build a bridge of your own.

You will need the Data sheet: Bridges.

Task 1

Use the Data sheet: Bridges to answer these questions.

1   How **long did it take** to **build** the Humber Bridge?

2   How many **vehicles** use the bridge each year?

3   How much **concrete** was used to build the Humber Bridge?

4   Which **two bridges** in the table on the sheet have the **same carriageway widths**?

5   A distance of **5 miles** is approximately equal to **8 kilometres**. How many kilometres **further** is it to travel from **Hull to Grimsby** by **motorway** rather than using the **bridge**?

6   For **how many years** was the Humber Bridge the **longest single-span suspension bridge** in the world?

7   How much **longer** is the span of the **Humber Bridge** than that of the **Golden Gate Bridge**?

8   How much **more** does it cost for a **car** than a **motorcycle** to cross the Humber Bridge?

9   In 2007, a total of **5 702 543** cars crossed the bridge. What was the **total amount paid** by the drivers of these cars?

10 What **percentage** of the **eight bridges** listed in the table is in China?

Learning objectives

Representing: decide which methods to use to make progress with the solution

Analysing: use appropriate mathematical procedures

Interpreting: test generalisations and draw conclusions from the mathematical analysis

Performing: analyse the situation or problem and decide which is the appropriate mathematical method needed to tackle it; give a solution to a practical problem, even if it is not within a familiar context, and make sure the solution is presented in a clear and understandable way

Links with
ICT, Geography, Science, Design and Technology

Task 2

Here are some facts about a **different** bridge. Use the information given in the table on the Data sheet to work out **which of the eight bridges** this is about. **Explain** how you worked out your answer.

> The steel for this bridge was made in **New Jersey**, **Maryland** and **Pennsylvania** and shipped through the **Panama Canal**.
>
> There are **128 lights** on the bridge roadway, which were installed in 1972.
>
> The bridge was closed on its **fiftieth** birthday.

Task 3

Design and build a **bridge** that has a **span** of **at least 30 centimetres**.

Draw up a **design specification** before you start to construct the bridge.

Your bridge should be **strong enough** to support the **weight of a calculator** at any point. Your bridge must be **at least 10 cm** above the ground at **all points between the supports**.

Your design specification should include any **measurements** that you make.

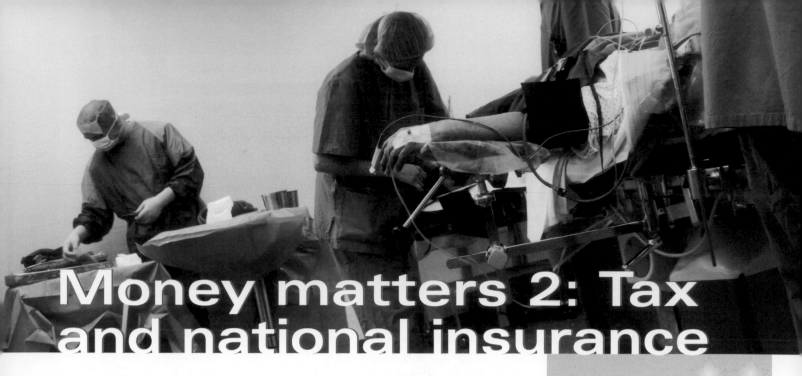

Money matters 2: Tax and national insurance

All workers who earn money have to pay income tax. Most people pay tax by the Pay as you earn (PAYE) system. This means tax is taken on wages each week or month, so that the worker does not get a huge tax bill once a year. Taxes are used to fund things such as the National Health Service (NHS), the armed forces, the police and government expenses. In addition, workers also pay national insurance contributions (NIC). These are used to cover pensions, sick pay and benefits.

The amount a worker earns, before any deductions are made, is called the gross income. The amount a worker receives is called the net income or take-home pay.

Each year the Government publishes a budget that sets all the tax rates and allowances.

Personal allowance

Everyone is allowed a personal tax allowance. This is the amount anyone is allowed to earn before they start paying income tax. The difference between gross income and personal tax allowance is the taxable income.

This is the tax allowance table for 2009–10.

Income tax allowance	2009–10
Personal allowance	£6475

Links with
ICT

Tax rates

Tax is charged at different rates, depending on how much a worker earns overall. There is a basic tax rate of 20% and a higher tax rate of 40% on taxable earnings over £34 800.

These rates apply to taxable income, not gross income.

This table shows the tax rate for 2009–10.

Tax rates on *taxable* income	2009–10
Basic rate: 20%	£0 – £37 400
Higher rate: 40%	Over £37 400

National insurance (NI)

The rate paid in national insurance varies, depending on total earnings. For everything between the primary threshold and the upper earning limits, a worker will pay 11% and for everything over the upper earnings limit the worker will pay 1% (2009 rates).

This table shows the NIC rate for 2009–10 for earnings per week.

	2009–10
Upper earnings limit	£844
Primary threshold	£110
Rate between primary threshold and upper earnings limit	11%
Rate above upper earnings limit	1%

Example 1

Mr T earns £380 per week. Work out his net income.

Answer

Gross income = £380 × 52 = £19 760 per annum

Taxable income = £19 760 − £6475 = £13 285

Tax paid = 20% of £13 285 = £2657

Weekly tax paid = £2657 ÷ 52 = £51.10

NI contribution = 11% of (£380 − £110) = £29.70

Net weekly income = £380 − (£51.10 + £29.70) = £299.20

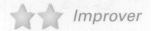

Example 2

Ms C earns £82 000 per annum. Work out her monthly take-home salary.

Answer

Monthly salary = £82 000 ÷ 12 = £6833.33

Taxable income = £82 000 − £6475 = £75 525

Tax paid = 20% of £37 400 + 40% of (£75 525 − £37 400) = 0.2 × £37 400 + 0.4 × £38 125 = £22 730

Monthly tax payable = £22 730 ÷ 12 = £1894.17

Weekly earnings = £82 000 ÷ 52 = £1576.92

NI contribution = 11% of £734 + 1% of (£1576.92 − £844) = £88.06

Monthly NI contribution = £88.06 × 52 ÷ 12 = £381.60

Net monthly income = £6833.33 − £1894.17 − £381.60 = £4557.56

Questions

1   Miss P earns **£220 per week**. Work out her **weekly take-home pay**.

2   Mr Q earns **£44 000 per annum**. Work out his **monthly net salary**.

3   Mrs R earns **£2500 per month**. Work out her **monthly net salary**.

4   Ms S earns **£550 per week**. Work out her **weekly net wage**.

5   Mr T earns **£380 per week**. His wife, Mrs T, earns **£130 per week**.
     Work out their **joint weekly take-home pay**.

6   Mr U earns **£52 000 a year**. His partner, Ms V, earns **£58 000 a year**. What is their **joint monthly net income**?

7   Mr W earns **£3000 a month**. Six months into the year he gets a pay rise of **£500 a month**. Work out by how much **extra** his take-home salary increases after the rise.

8   Mr X earns **£2000 per month**. He pays taxes and national insurance at the **normal rates** for **8 months**. He is then made redundant and doesn't get another job for the rest of the year.

    a   Work out how much **tax he would pay** on an annual income of **£24 000**.
    b   Work out how much **tax he would pay** on an annual income of **£16 000**.
    c   Work out how much **tax rebate he should get** at the **end of the year**.

Revision planning

As you approach exams, you may decide to plan for revision so that you can do as well as possible. In this activity, you will make revision plans for two students and for yourself.

This table shows the subjects that the students are taking.

Core subjects
English
Mathematics
Science

Other subjects
Design and technology
French
Geography
History
ICT
Media studies
Music
PE

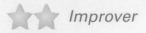

Task 1

Suppose you are a student in **Year 11** and you are **planning revision** for your examinations.

You need to plan a **7-day revision programme**. Include **all of the subjects** listed above.

Each day you have up to **six half-hour revision slots** to fill.

You have already decided that **core subjects** will have **2 hours per week** and **other subjects** will have **1 hour per week**.

For any **core subject**, you should revise for no **more than 1 hour per day** (two slots together or two separate slots).

For **other subjects**, you should revise for **no more than $\frac{1}{2}$ hour per day**.

You **should not revise** any **core subject** immediately **after another core subject**. (Ignore breaks.)

This plan will leave you **7 hours free** for **other activities**.

You could use a chart like this to create your timetable.

	6.00 pm–6.30 pm	6.30 pm–7.00 pm	7.00 pm–7.15 pm	7.15 pm–7.45 pm	7.45 pm–8.15 pm	8.15 pm–8.30 pm	8.30 pm–9.00 pm	9.00 pm–9.30 pm
Monday								
Tuesday								
Wednesday			Break			Break		
Thursday								
Friday								
Saturday								
Sunday								

Task 2

Now suppose you decide to do even more revision. You will still use up to six half-hour slots each **weekday** (Monday to Friday) but you decide that on **Saturday and Sunday** you will use **up to six 45-minute slots** with **30-minute breaks**.

Your **weekend** revision will start at **10.00 am each day**.

You have up to **six half-hour revision slots** to fill on each **weekday** (Monday to Friday) and up to **six 45-minute slots** to fill on **Saturday and Sunday**.

Copy the tables opposite. Complete the timings in the table for **Saturday and Sunday**, starting from **10.00 am** each day. Now fill in your timetable using the following rules.

You have decided that:

- **core subjects** will have **3 hours per week**
- **French** will have **2 hours per week**
- **history** will have **1.5 hours per week**
- **other subjects** will have **1 hour per week**.

You should revise **any core subject** for **no more than**:

- **1 hour per day** (two slots together or two separate slots) on **weekdays**
- **1.5 hours per day** (two slots together or two separate slots) on **Saturday or Sunday**.

You should revise **other subjects** for **no more than**:

- $\frac{1}{2}$ **hour per day** on **weekdays**
- **45 minutes** on **Saturdays or Sundays**.

You **should not revise** any **core subject** immediately **after another core subject**. (Ignore breaks.)

This will leave you **5.5 hours free** for **other activities**.

	6.00 pm–6.30 pm	6.30 pm–7.00 pm	7.00 pm–7.15 pm	7.15 pm–7.45 pm	7.45 pm 8.15 pm	8.15 pm–8.30 pm	8.30 pm–9.00 pm	9.00 pm–9.30 pm
Monday			Break			Break		
Tuesday								
Wednesday								
Thursday								
Friday								

	10.00 am–							
Saturday								
Sunday								

Task 3

Using your own subjects, make up your own revision rules and plan your own revision timetable.

At the gym

A gym opens from 6 am to 8 pm each day from Monday to Friday and from 9 am to 5 pm on Saturday and Sunday.

In the men's changing rooms at the gym there is a shower room with five showers.

The diagram shows the plan of the shower room.

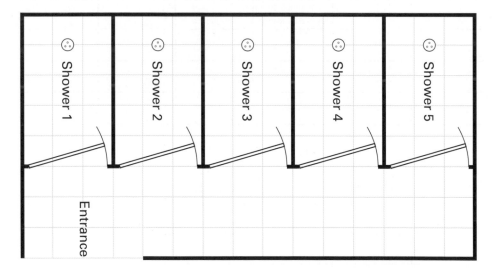

Shower 1

Shower 2

Shower 3

Shower 4

Shower 5

Entrance

Each shower is equipped with a soap dispenser that holds 500 ml of soap when full.

The dispensers are filled every morning, before the gym opens. At 9 am one of the staff checks the dispensers.

Learning objectives

Representing: recognise that a real-life problem can be solved using appropriate mathematics

Interpreting: interpret results and solutions and make a generalisation about them; check that a conclusion is appropriate and accurate in the context of the original problem

Performing: use mathematical skills and knowledge to make progress on a real-life problem, even if the situation described is not a familiar context; draw a conclusion from working and provide a mathematical justification for this conclusion

This diagram shows the level in each dispenser at 9 am one Monday.

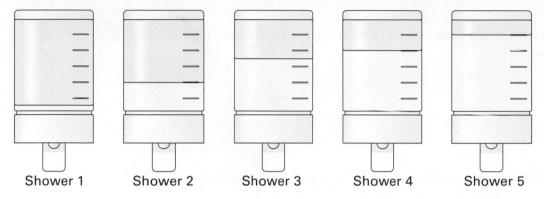

| Shower 1 | Shower 2 | Shower 3 | Shower 4 | Shower 5 |

This is the distribution of men entering the gym for that day.

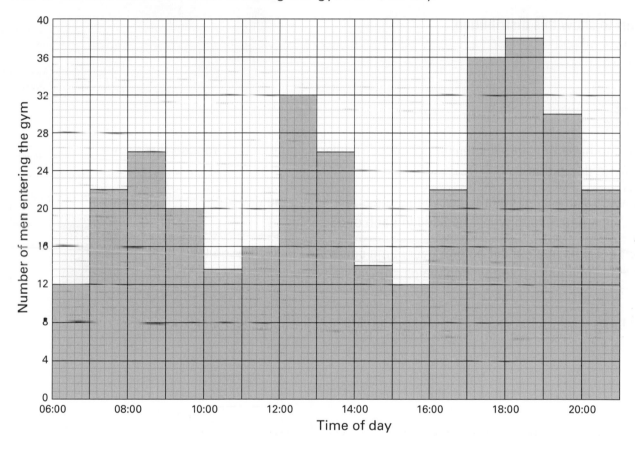

Task 1

Give an explanation for the **levels of soap** in **each dispenser** at **9 am**.

Task 2

Give an explanation for the **distribution of men entering the gym** during the day.

Task 3

Work out approximately **how much soap** will be used in the men's showers on this day.
Give your answer in **litres**.

Task 4

The manager describes the **distribution** of men in the gym on Saturday like this.

> *'There are about 20 members each hour entering the gym, with a slight increase over lunchtime and in the early afternoon.'*

Draw a **bar chart** to show this **distribution**.

Task 5

The manager has to have the soap dispensers checked regularly and wants to **reduce the time** her staff spend doing this.

Please use shower

a   If all showers were used **equally** between 6 am and 9 am on the day in question, how much soap would be used in each one?

b   The manager puts in a sensor so that every time someone walks through the entrance a sign lights up suggesting which shower they should use.

The following Monday, when the showers are checked at 9 am these are the levels of soap in the dispensers.

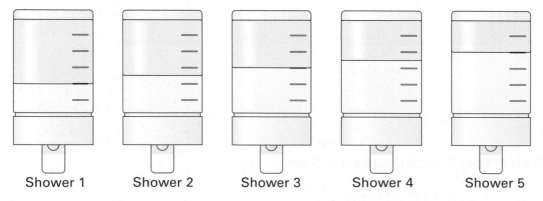

| Shower 1 | Shower 2 | Shower 3 | Shower 4 | Shower 5 |

Given that the **distribution** of men entering the gym **is the same as for the previous Monday**, work out the **latest time** the manager should get the dispensers checked so that **none of them runs out**.

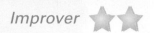

Task 6 (extension)

To stay healthy an average man needs 2500 calories and an average woman needs 2000 calories a day.

Moderate cycling on the exercise bike, moderate rowing on the rowing machine, aerobics, using the treadmill at walking pace and light weightlifting will burn about 7 calories per minute.

Fast cycling on the exercise bike, heavy rowing on the rowing machine, kick boxing, using the treadmill at jogging pace and heavy weightlifting will burn about 10 calories per minute.

Design an exercise program that last one hour and burns approximately 500 calories.

Use the internet to find out how many calories various sportsmen use

For example

- Riders in the Tour de France each day
- Marathon runners during a marathon
- Professional footballers during a match

Money matters 3: Loans and APR

Almost always, when someone takes out a loan they have to pay interest.

Companies that offer credit and loans must always state the interest rate they charge, and this is usually given as the annual percentage rate (APR).

The APR shows what your interest payment would be if the interest was compounded and paid annually instead of monthly (or any other period). The APR is used so that customers can compare different credit and loan deals.

When the APR is calculated it takes into account the interest the customer has to pay, the timing and amount of the payments, any fees for setting up the deal, and any fees for payment protection if the lender makes this compulsory.

The law says that all lenders must tell you what their APR is before you sign an agreement.

Generally, the lower the APR the better the deal for the customer.

Look at these advertisements for loans.

TopService Personal Loans

The typical rate is 7.8% APR on all loans from £5000 to £25 000

Apply online for a TS loan.

Monthly repayments.

Gordon's cheap loans

Wipe out debt. Get a loan. Call in today.

Borrow from £5000 to £100 000

Consolidate all your debts into 1 lower monthly payment

Raise money for home improvements, a holiday, etc

Borrow up to 80% of your property value.

APR from as low as 8.5%

The Instant Cash Loans Company

One-off payment option.

Borrow cash now up to £1000.

Pay back on pay-day.

One simple phone call away.

You receive	Our interest	Repayable
£80.00	£20.00	£100.00
£160.00	£40.00	£200.00
£240.00	£60.00	£300.00
£320.00	£80.00	£400.00
£400.00	£100.00	£500.00

APR 1284% based on 31 days

The Lending Bank

You can borrow up to £20 000.
You can choose from fixed monthly repayments of one to five years.
Enjoy the peace of mind of our optional loan repayment insurance.

APR 9.9%

Apply online or call at your local branch.

£££££££££

Cash Around the Corner Loans

Apply now for cash loans from £50 to £500 with no hidden charges

Your local loan shop, established 100 years

Example:
Loan amount: £100, 57 weekly repayments of £3 Total amount payable £171
189.2% APR

Example 1

Calculate the APR on **a loan of £1000** for **one year** at **10% interest**, repaid at the **end of the year**.

Answer

Interest = 10% of £1000 = £100

Total repayment at the end of the year = £1100

The APR is 10%.

Example 2

Calculate the APR on a **loan of £1000** for **one year** at **10% interest**, **repaid every month** in **equal monthly instalments**.

10% interest = 10% of £1000 = £100

Total repayment made throughout the year = £1100

Because the money is paid back throughout the year, not all of the £1100 is available for the whole year, so the APR is much higher. It is about 20%.

Warm-up questions

1   Look at the advertisement for **TopService Loans**.

   a What is the **least** you can **borrow**?

   b What is the **most** you can **borrow**?

   c How much is **7.8%** of **£1000**?

   d How much is **7.8%** of **£5000**?

2   Look at the advertisement for **Gordon's Cheap Loans**.

   a How **often** are the **repayments**?

   b If you own a property worth **£100 000**, what is the **most** that can you borrow?

   c How much is **8.5%** of **£10 000**?

   d How much is **8.5%** of **£50 000**?

3   Look at the advertisement for **The Instant Cash Loans Company**.

   a How much is the **APR** (based on **31 days**)?

   b What is **£20** as a **percentage** of **£80**?

   c Why is the **APR** so **high**?

4   Look at the advertisement for **Cash Around the Corner Loans**.

   a How **often** are the **repayments**?

   b What is the **most** you can borrow?

   c Why is this **APR** so **high**?

5 Look at the advertisement for **The Lending Bank**.

    a What is **most** that you can borrow?

    b What is the **longest time** you can take to **pay off the loan**?

    c **What else** do they offer to go with the loan?

Task 1

Copy and complete the table. The first company has been done for you.

Name of company	Online, branch or shop	Amount that can be borrowed	Repayments: one payment, weekly or monthly	APR
TopService Personal Loans	Online	£5000 to £25 000	Monthly	7.8%
Gordon's Cheap Loans				
The Instant Cash Loans Company				
Cash Around the Corner Loans				
The Lending Bank				

Task 2

Imagine that you wanted to take out a **loan**.

Prepare a report **analysing** the advertisements shown.

For each advertisement, state any **good points** or any **bad points**.

Explain which are **easy** to follow.

Design your own advertisement, using the **best features** of the advertisements shown.

Stickers

Lots of companies sell packs of stickers, for example, of football clubs or the Harry Potter books and films. Collectors buy them in packs and stick them into albums until they have collected a **full set**. The packs are put together **randomly** so nobody knows in advance what stickers will be in the pack. Most people end up with several stickers the same, just missing a couple of stickers to complete the set. There are internet sites where stickers can be bought or swapped.

In this activity you will build a **mathematical model** to study the process of completing a set of stickers.

Task 1

This task will model how long it takes to get a full set of stickers when there are a **total of five** to collect and they are sold in **packs of three**.

Work in pairs or small groups.

Take a sheet of A4 card and divide it into **20 equal rectangles**, five rows and four columns.

Now decide what your sticker set is going to be about.

You will need to have **five different things** or **people** in your set. For example, you can choose five of your favourite pop artists or just five colours.

The cards shown in the example are marked H, M, B, L and Mg. Can you guess what these represent? Your teacher will tell you later if you don't guess straight away.

Mark **each** thing or person on **four** of the cards.

Learning objectives

Representing: decide which methods to use to make progress with the solution

Analysing: establish a pattern or relationship and then change the variables to see how this changes the results

Interpreting: interpret results and solutions and make a generalisation about them; test generalisations and draw conclusions from the mathematical analysis; check that a conclusion is appropriate and accurate in the context of the original problem

Performing: use mathematical skills and knowledge to make progress on a problem, even if it does not use a routine mathematical procedure; analyse the situation or problem and decide which is the appropriate mathematical method needed to tackle it; use a range of mathematics to find solutions

Links with
ICT

Now cut the cards out carefully, so all of them are **exactly the same shape and size**.

Turn the cards over and **shuffle them** or lay them out on the table and mix them up, so you can't see what is on the front.

Now choose **three cards at random** and write down what you get.

Put the cards back, face down, **shuffle them again** and take **three more cards at random**. Again, note the cards you get.

Keep on doing this until you have picked one of each type.

Each time you pick a **set of three cards** it represents buying a **pack of stickers**.

For example:

Pack 1   H, L, L   So far you have collected H and L.
Pack 2   M, L, H   So far you have collected M, H and L.
Pack 3   Mg, H, M   So far you have collected M, H, L and Mg.
Pack 4   M, H, H   So far you have collected M, H, L and Mg.
Pack 5   M, B, H   Now you have collected the whole set M, H, L, Mg and B.

This has modelled the situation where it took **five packs** to collect a **whole set**.

Repeat this task **five times** in total.

What was the **smallest number** of packs it took to get a whole set?
What was the **greatest number** of packs it took to get a whole set?
What was the **average number** of packs it took to get a whole set?

Your teacher may collect in the results from **all groups** and work out an **average** for the **whole class**.

Task 2

It is generally claimed, but denied by the companies that make stickers, that they do not print exactly the same number of each sticker in the set.

This task will model how long it takes to get a full set of stickers when there are a total of **five to collect** and they are sold in **packs of three** but where the **numbers of each type of sticker printed are not equal**.

Proceed as before but, this time, only mark **two cards with H**, mark **three with M**, mark **four with B**, mark **five with L** and mark **six with Mg**.

Repeat the experiment, again taking **three cards at a time** until you have a **full set**.

Repeat this task **five times in total**.

What was the **smallest number** of packs it took to get a whole set?

What was the **greatest number** of packs it took to get a whole set?

What was the **average number** of packs it took to get a whole set?

You should have found it took **a lot longer** to get a full set.

Task 3 (extension)

Now make up your own mathematical model for the **total number of stickers in a set** and the **number of stickers in a pack,** using a computer **spreadsheet** program.

Imagine there are **20 stickers in total in the set** and they are sold in **packs of four**.

Open up a blank spreadsheet and in cell A1 type in **=INT((RAND() * 20) + 1)**, then press **return**. Copy this formula down **column A** for about **20 rows**. Now highlight all the cells with numbers in **column A** and copy this across for **four columns**.

This should look something like the screen below (without the circles).

	A	B	C	D
1	5	10	4	13
2	9	15	4	7
3	16	2	14	19
4	2	1	16	5
5	16	20	13	19
6	16	2	19	20
7	20	17	4	3
8	7	14	1	7
9	9	20	10	4
10	4	16	20	1
11	12	15	18	2
12	2	19	16	20
13	12	10	14	3
14	7	3	3	11
15	5	12	1	9
16	2	5	1	15
17	7	4	7	14
18	7	17	15	10
19	11	4	5	14
20	7	17	12	14

> This model was for **20 stickers in packs of four**. If it had been for **25 stickers in packs of five**, the spreadsheet formula would be **=INT((RAND() * 25) + 1)** and the formula would be copied across for **five rows**.

The circles show the numbers **from 1 to 20**. So **even after 20 packs** have been bought there is still not a complete set as **6 and 8 are missing**. The formula would need to be **copied down for more rows** until 6 and 8 are obtained.

Imagine **sticker packs cost £1 each**. How much will it **cost** to **complete a set**?

Money matters 4: Savings and AER

The annual equivalent rate (AER) is the interest rate quoted on interest paid on savings and investments.

It shows what the interest return would be if the interest was compounded and paid annually instead of monthly (or any other period).

The AER is used so that customers can compare different savings accounts.

Gross AER is the rate of interest before deduction of income tax.

Net AER is the amount of interest payable after deduction of 20% tax for basic-rate taxpayers.

Here are some advertisements for savings accounts.

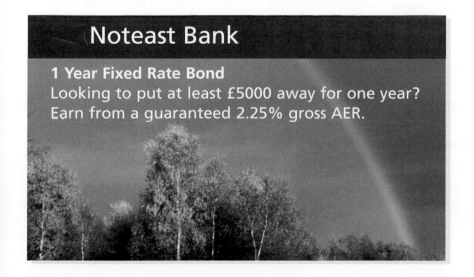

Noteast Bank

1 Year Fixed Rate Bond
Looking to put at least £5000 away for one year?
Earn from a guaranteed 2.25% gross AER.

Monastery
BUILDING SOCIETY

eSaver Direct

Committed online savers will enjoy a great variable rate of 2.30% gross/AER if you make just one withdrawal in the first year or 2.50% gross/AER if you make none. This includes a bonus of 0.75% gross/AER for 12 months.

A lower interest rate of 0.10% gross/AER applies for each calendar month in which a withdrawal takes place.

WINDSOR BUILDING SOCIETY

The minimum balance for this account is £500.

A fixed interest rate of 1.50% Gross/AER is payable.

No penalty for withdrawals.

BRADLEY BANK

£1000+ invested. 3.00% gross pa/AER (variable) including 1.40% bonus (gross) for 12 months.

Bonus of 1.40% (gross) paid for first 12 months provided you maintain a balance of at least £1000.

Charnal Building Society

1, 2 or 3 Year Fixed Term Bond

Annual:		
3.00% Gross pa	2.40% Net pa	3.00% AER
Monthly:		
2.96% Gross pa	2.37% Net pa	3.00% AER

Interest rates are fixed until:
1-Year Option Fixed Term
2-Year Option Fixed Term
3-Year Option Fixed Term

Interest applies to balances of £1 plus.

A **withdrawal penalty** equivalent to 180 days' loss of interest on the amount withdrawn applies for the fixed-rate period.

Warm-up questions

1   Look at the advertisement for the **Noteast Bank**.

   a   From the information given, what is a **fixed rate bond**?

   b   Is it possible to invest **£2000** in this bond?

   c   How much is **2.25%** of **£1000**?

   d   How much is **2.25%** of **£5000**?

2   Look at the advertisement for the **Monastery Building Society**.

    a   Where do you **invest** in this account?

    b   What is the **interest rate** without **withdrawals** (AER)?

    c   What is the **interest rate** in a month when a **withdrawal** takes place (AER)?

3   Look at advertisement for the **Windsor Building Society**.

    a   How much do you need to **invest** in this account?

    b   What is the **interest rate** (AER)?

    c   What is the **penalty** for **withdrawals**?

4   Look at advertisement for the **Bradley Bank**.

    a   What is the **least amount** that you can **invest** in this account?

    b   When is the **bonus paid**?

5   Look at advertisement for the **Charnal Building Society**.

    a   What is the **penalty** for **withdrawals**?

    b   How much do you need to **invest** to receive **interest**?

    c   What does **net pa** mean?

Task 1

Some accounts have **restrictions** on whether you can invest in them.

For each account, if possible, work out the **annual interest** for an investment of

    a   £500

    b   £1000

    c   £5000

Where it is not possible to invest the sum of money, explain the reason why.

Assume that no withdrawals are made.

Task 2

Imagine that you are the marketing manager of a different building society or bank.

Prepare a **report**, analysing the advertisements shown.

For each advertisement, state any **good points** or any **bad points**.

Explain which advertisements are **easy to follow**.

Design **your own advertisement**, using the **best features** of those shown.

Shuffleboard

Shuffleboard is a game in which players take turns to propel red or yellow discs along the playing area. Each player shoots four discs. Points are scored when the discs land in the areas marked with numbers in the scoring triangle.

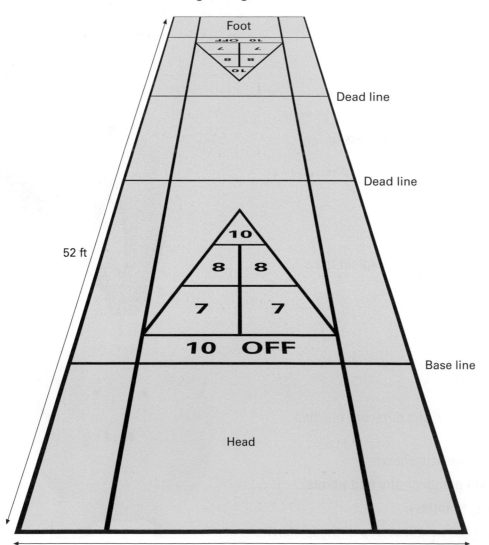

Foot

10 OFF

7 | 7

8 | 8

10

Dead line

Dead line

10

8 | 8

7 | 7

10 OFF

Base line

52 ft

Head

10 ft

This is a plan view of the scoring triangle. It is drawn to scale with 1 square representing 1 foot.

Possible scores are 10, 8, 7 and 10 off, which means a disc landing in this area causes 10 points to be deducted from the player's total.

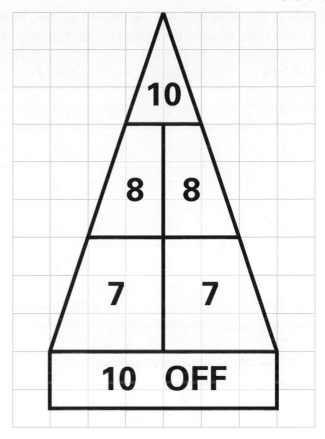

Task 1

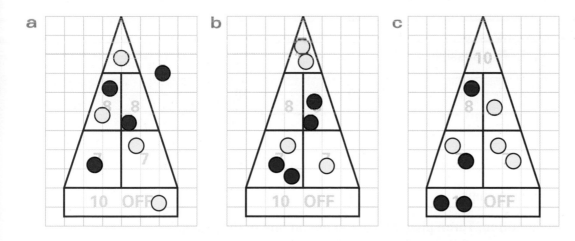

a

b

c

Work out the **scores** for the **red** and **yellow discs** in these diagrams.

Task 2

A score of 4 is the **lowest possible positive score**. This can be obtained by scoring **0, 7, 7** and **–10**. **Zero** (0) means the **disc does not score**.

Scores of **5, 6, 7** and **8** are also **possible** but a score of **9** is **impossible**.

The **maximum possible score** would be **40**, with four scores of 10.

Complete the table below to see which scores, **from 4 to 40**, are possible. There may be more than one answer for some scores. You only need to find one.

Score	Disc 1	Disc 2	Disc 3	Disc 4
4	0	7	7	−10
5	0	7	8	−10
6	0	8	8	−10
7	0	0	0	7
8	0	0	0	8
9	Not possible			
10				
11				

38	10	10	10	8
39	Not possible			
40	10	10	10	10

Task 3

Shuffleboard is very popular on cruise ships.

Two teams decide to have a **competition**. **Three players** want to get on one of the teams. They each record their scores for at least their last **30** games.

Alf records his scores in a **stem-and-leaf diagram**.

Key: 1 | 2 represents a score of 12

```
0 |  7   8
1 |  4   5   5   6   6   7   7   8   8
2 |  0   1   1   2   2   3   4   5   7   8   8   8
3 |  0   0   1   1   2   3   4
```

Brenda records her scores in a **grouped table**.

Score	Frequency
16 ⩽ score ⩽ 20	9
21 ⩽ score ⩽ 25	18
26 ⩽ score ⩽ 30	3

Clara records her scores as a **frequency diagram** like this.

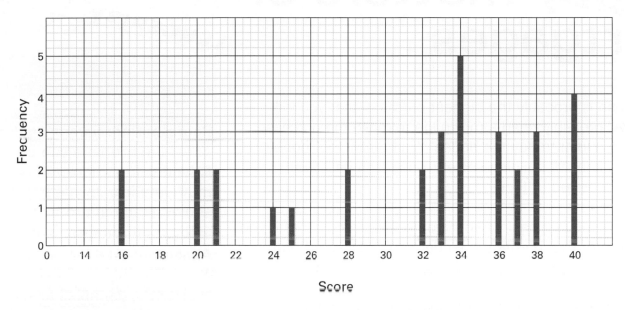

You are the team captain.

   a   Explain **fully** why you would pick **Clara** for the team.

   b   **Who** would you pick as the **reserve**? **Why**?

Task 4 (extension)

The scoring triangle consists of an **isosceles triangle**, **four trapezia** and a **rectangle**.

Work out the **area** of **each of these shapes**.

Assuming that where the disc lands is random, calculate the **probability** of each score by working out the **area of each score** as a **decimal fraction** of the **total area**.

Money matters 5: Mortgages

Buying a house is probably the biggest purchase that you will make. You will probably need a mortgage to make the purchase. A mortgage is a loan to buy the house. You borrow the money, usually from a bank or building society, and pay it back, with interest, over a period of time.

Mortgages are secured against your home. This means that if you cannot afford the repayments the lender could sell your home to get their money back.

Although there are many different types of mortgage, the most common is the repayment mortgage.

Repayment mortgage

The amount you pay each month is made up of capital (some of the amount you borrowed) and interest.

The amount is calculated so that you are guaranteed to have repaid everything you owe by the end of the borrowing period.

Example 1

You **borrow £100 000** at **5% interest** for **20 years**.
The **monthly repayment** = £659.96
The **interest paid** = £58 390.40

Example 2

You **borrow £100 000** at **4% interest** for **25 years**.
The **monthly repayment** = £527.84
The **interest paid** = £58 352.00

Example 3

You **borrow £100 000** at **6% interest** for **10 years**.
The **monthly repayment** = £1110.21
The **interest paid** = £ 33 225.19

Variable rate and fixed rate mortgages

Mortgages may also be variable rate or fixed-rate.

If you have a variable rate mortgage, the lender can change the interest rate, which means the cost of your mortgage can go up or down.

If you have a fixed rate mortgage, the lender fixes the interest rate for an agreed period of time, usually for the first one, two or three years, and then changes the arrangement, either to a variable rate or to offer a new fixed rated.

This table shows the advantages and disadvantages of a fixed rate mortgage.

Advantages	Disadvantages
You know exactly how much you will have to pay for the whole period of time.	You will probably pay more than the variable rate on offer at the beginning.
You are not affected by interest rate rises.	You are not affected by interest rate falls.

Task 1

The table shows the **monthly repayments** for an **interest rate of 5%**.

	£110 000	£120 000	£130 000	£140 000	£150 000
15 years	£883.14	£963.42	£1043.71	£1123.99	£1204.28
20 years	£735.56	£802.43	£869.29	£936.16	£1003.03
25 years	£650.40	£709.52	£768.65	£827.78	£886.91

1   How much is the **monthly repayment** for a **£120 000** mortgage taken out for **20 years**?

2   How much is the **monthly repayment** for a **£150 000** mortgage taken out for **15 years**?

3   How much would be the **total repaid** for a **£110 000** mortgage taken out for **25 years**?

4   How much would be the **total repaid** for a **£140 000** mortgage taken out for **15 years**?

5 How much **more** does it cost per **month** for a **£120 000** mortgage than a **£150 000** mortgage taken out for **20 years**?

This table shows the **monthly repayments** for an **interest rate of 7%**.

	£110 000	£120 000	£130 000	£140 000	£150 000
15 years	£1006.45	£1097.95	£1189.44	£1280.94	£1372.43
20 years	£865.27	£943.93	£1022.59	£1101.25	£1179.91
25 years	£786.60	£858.11	£929.61	£1001.12	£1072.63

6 How much **more** is the **monthly repayment** for a **£130 000** mortgage taken out for **20 years** at **7%** than at **5%**?

7 How much **more** is the **monthly repayment** for a **£140 000** mortgage taken out for **25 years** at **7%** than at **5%**?

8 How much **more** would be the **total repaid** for a **£140 000** mortgage taken out for **15 years** at **7%** than **5%**?

9 Suppose you want a mortgage for **£300 000**.

Use the table to work out the **difference** in the **monthly repayments** for a **15-year** and a **20-year** mortgage with an interest rate of **7%**.

10 Suppose you want a mortgage for **£270 000**.

Use the table to work out the **monthly repayments** for a **25-year** mortgage.

Task 2

Do an internet search on **mortgage calculator**. Many different companies provide mortgage calculators but they all work in a similar way. When you find a mortgage calculator put in some details. For example:

Enter mortgage details

Mortgage amount (£)	100,000
Years left on mortgage	25
Annual rate of interest (%)	7

Monthly repayment

| 583.33 | Interest only |
| 706.78 | Repayment |

(Calculate)   (Clear)

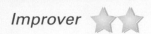

You can also use the **second part** of the calculator to find out what will happen if the **rate of interest increases**. You would need to know if you could still afford the mortgage.

What if the interest rate changes?

Would you still be able to pay? Select an interest rate to find out.

Choose rate increase	**Monthly repayment**

Rate increase   3%   883.33   Interest only

908.70   Repayment

(Recalculate)   (Clear)

Find a calculator that will compare mortgages when the **interest rate changes** as above.

Compare the **monthly repayments** for **different mortgages**.

Find out how **monthly repayments** for **different mortgages** change when the **interest rate changes**.

Prepare a **report** to present to the class. Make sure that you **comment** on the effect of:

- taking out a mortgage **for a longer period**
- **borrowing more**
- **increases** in the **interest rate**, for example, comment on the effect of a **1% increase** on a mortgage of **£100 000** taken over **25 years**.

Task 3

Advertisements for mortgages have to include the following warning statement.

> **Your home may be repossessed if you do not keep up repayments.**

Design your own **advertisement** for a **mortgage**. Give as much **information** as you can making all the facts as **clear** as possible.

Make sure that you:

- tell them **who you are**
- give **contact details** (make these up)
- state whether it is **fixed rate** or **variable rate**
  - If **fixed rate** state what happens to the interest rate **at the end of the fixed rate period**.
  - Does it revert to **variable rate**, is a **new fixed rate offered** or are **both options** available?
- state the **interest rate**
- state the **period** of the mortgage available (this could be a range, for example, 15 to 25 years).

Remember to include the **warning statement**.

Time zones

As you know from your science lessons, the Earth rotates on its axis. Therefore, sunrise occurs at different times in different parts of the world.

Because every part of the world considers that the day begins when they see the Sun rise, the Earth is divided into 24 time zones. This is why when it is 12 noon (midday) in London it is only 7 am in New York but 3 pm in Moscow. Businesses that trade with foreign countries need to be aware of the time differences so they can contact people when they are also at work. Travellers need to know about time differences so that they can plan journeys.

Time zones are based on Coordinated Universal Time (UTC). Previously, time zones were based on Greenwich Mean Time (GMT) but UTC has been used since 1961. In Britain, for all everyday purposes, time is based on GMT from the last Sunday in October to the last Sunday in March. For the rest of the year British Summer Time is used, which is equivalent to GMT + 1 or UTC + 1. Note that GMT and UTC do not vary throughout the year.

Times in most places around the world are whole numbers of hours ahead or behind UTC but in some places the difference may be in half or quarter hours.

The standard way of showing a time zone is UTC $\pm n$ (or GMT $\pm n$), where n is the difference in hours. For example, the local time at various places at 12:00 midday UTC would be:

- Los Angeles, California, United States: UTC − 8 = 04:00
- New York City, United States: UTC − 5 = 07:00
- London, United Kingdom, in December: UTC = 12:00
- Paris, France: UTC + 1 = 13:00
- Moscow, Russia: UTC + 3 = 15:00
- Karachi, Pakistan: UTC + 5 = 17:00

Learning objectives

Representing: recognise that a real-life problem can be solved using appropriate mathematics

Analysing: find a result or solution to the original problem

Performing: give a conclusion or answer to the original problem, using language and forms of representation that make sense to a wider population

Interpreting: give a solution to a practical problem, even if it is not within a familiar context and make sure the solution is presented in a clear and understandable way

Links with
Science, ICT and Geography

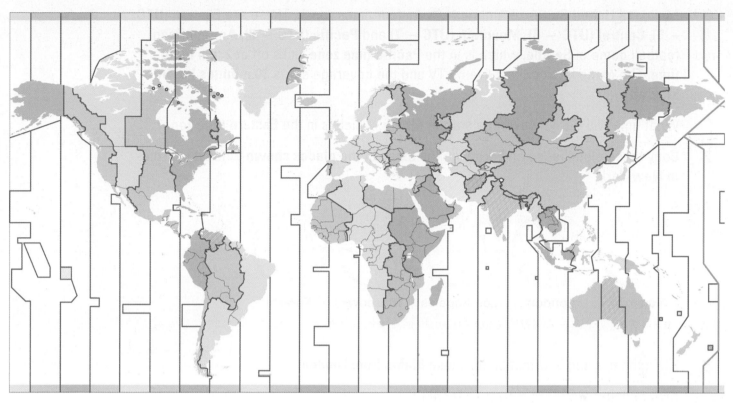

This map shows the time zones around the world.

Questions

1   A flight from **London to New York** takes **6 hours and 30 minutes**. It takes off from London at **8:30 am**. What will be the **local time** in **New York** when it lands?

2   A woman is in **Moscow** on business. She rings her family in the **United Kingdom** at **7 pm local time** in **Moscow**. What time does her family get the call?

3   A woman travels from **Los Angeles** to **Paris**. She leaves home in **Los Angeles** at **midday local time** and arrives at her sister's house in **Paris** at **5.30 pm local time** the **following day**. How long did her journey take, door to door?

4   A business has offices in New York, London and Paris.

   The **New York** office is open from **8 am to 6 pm** local time.

   The **London** office is open from **9 am to 5 pm** local time.

   The **Paris** office is open from **10 am to 7 pm** local time.

   For how many hours in the day are **all three offices open** at the **same time**?

5   The time in **Melbourne**, Australia is **UTC + 11**. At **9 am local time** Mr Dundee, who lives in **London**, rings his daughter in Melbourne to wish her a happy Christmas. What time of the day does **his daughter** get the call?

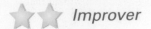

6   Mainland United States of America covers four times zones. These are **Eastern (UTC – 5)**, **Central (UTC – 6)**, **Mountain (UTC – 7)** and **Pacific (UTC – 8)**. An American football game in Seattle, which is in the **Pacific time zone** kicks off at **2 pm local time**. The game is broadcast live on TV and the coverage starts **30 minutes before kick off**.

What time will the TV coverage start in **Miami**, which is in the **Eastern time zone**?

7   Copy these clock faces and draw on the **times in the places shown** when it is **1 pm in New York**.

| New York | London | Los Angeles | Moscow | Karachi |

8   Fill in the missing information for these **flights from London**.

Arrival times are always given in **local time**.

Flight	Destination	Departure	Length of flight	Arrival Time
AU1	Moscow	06:45	3 h 10 m	
AU2	Paris	10:25	1 h 05 m	
AU3	New York	11:10		14:30
AU4	Los Angeles	08:50		10:20
AU5	Karachi		8 h 15 m	20:30

9   A family arranges a three-way video call on New Year's Eve. Laura is in **Melbourne (UTC + 11)**, Andrew is in **Newcastle (UTC + 0)** and Carol is in **Miami (UTC – 5)**. Laura makes the call **five minutes before midnight, local time**. What are the **local times** for Andrew and Carol?

10   A family in Vancouver, **Canada, (UTC – 8)** listens to a BBC radio programme **live** on the internet. The program is broadcast in the **UK** from **8 pm to 10 pm**. Between what **local times** will the family listen to the programme in **Vancouver**?

Planning a bedroom

Imagine you are moving to a new house, where you will need to plan how you want your bedroom.

For each task below, the scale drawing represents a bedroom. The plan shows the position of the door and any windows.

You need to decide how to fit out the bedroom with new furniture. First, you will need to decide what size of bed to put in the room. You will also need to include sufficient wardrobes and drawers to make the room practical to use.

Use centimetre-squared graph paper to draw up your own scale drawing for the plan for each bedroom. Choose a scale so that your diagram takes up the whole sheet of graph paper.

Write a brief report explaining any decisions you take. For example, say why you chose the position of the furniture and other items and explain the number of drawers you wanted.

The Data sheet: Planning a bedroom gives details of furniture sizes.

Learning objectives

Representing: recognise that a real-life problem can be solved using appropriate mathematics

Analysing: use appropriate mathematical procedures; find a result or solution to the original problem

Interpreting: check that a conclusion is appropriate and accurate in the context of the original problem; give a conclusion or answer to the original problem, using language and forms of presentation that make sense to a wider population

Performing: use mathematical skills and knowledge to make progress on a real-life problem, even if the situation described is not within a familiar context; check work and methods when tackling a problem and decide if a different approach may be more effective

Links with
Design and technology, ICT

Task 1

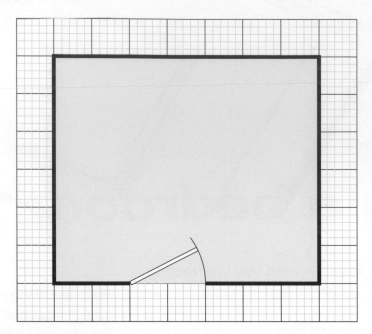

Scale: 1 centimetre represents 0.5 metres

Task 2

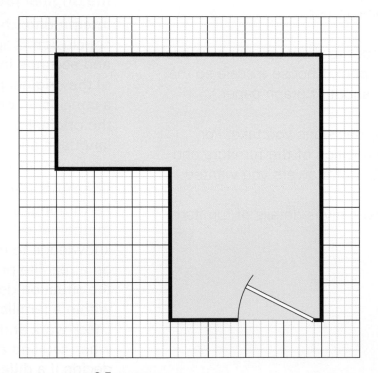

Scale: 1 centimetre represents 0.5 metres

Task 3

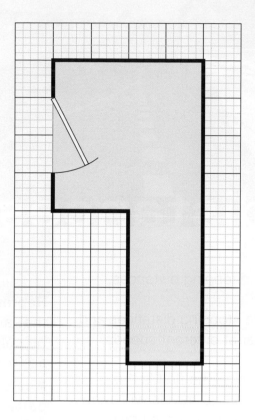

Scale: 1 centimetre represents 0.5 metres

Stopping distances

For this activity you will need Data sheet: Stopping distances.

The *Highway Code* includes a table of safe stopping distances and gives advice to drivers about stopping a car at different speeds.

The stopping distance consists of two phases. The first is the thinking distance. This is the distance the vehicle travels while the driver's brain reacts to the situation and realises that the brake needs to be applied. The second phase is the braking distance, which is the distance the vehicle travels before it comes to a stop.

Data sheet: Stopping distances shows the stopping distances for various speeds.

Task 1

1   How many **kilometres** are equivalent to **10 miles**?

2   What is the **thinking distance** for a speed of **50 mph**?

3   What is the **braking distance** for a speed of **96 km/h**?

4   What is the **total stopping distance** for a speed of **40 mph**?

5   What is the **total stopping distance** for a speed of **112 km/h**?

6   Estimate the **thinking distance** for a speed of **45 mph**.

7   Estimate the **total stopping distance** for a speed of **65 mph**.

8   How many **car lengths** should be left between cars travelling at **70 mph** to be totally safe?

9 The graph shows the **thinking distance** (blue), **braking distance** (red) and **total stopping distance** (black) for cars travelling at **20 mph** and **30 mph**. Copy and complete the graph.

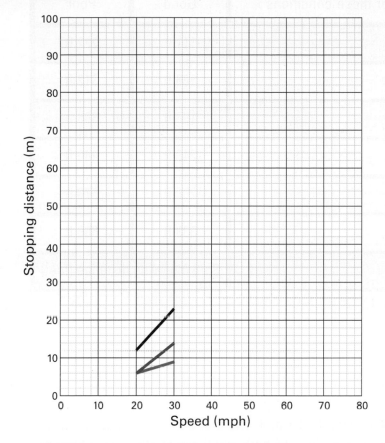

10 The **maximum speed limit** in Britain is **70 mph**. Extend the graph to estimate the **thinking**, **braking** and **total stopping distances** for **80 mph**.

Task 2

The table on the next page, from an American website, recommends leaving a **3-second gap** between cars in **good driving conditions** and a **6-second gap** in **poor driving conditions**.

1 Work out the **middle distances** for each pair, to get the distance travelled at **30 mph**, **40 mph**, **50 mph**, **60 mph** and **70 mph** for both a **3-second** and **6-second** gap.

2 There are **3.25 feet** in **1 metre**. Convert the distances in question 1 to **metres**. Give your answers to the **nearest metre**.

3 Compare **these distances** to those based on the **UK stopping distances**.

4 Another website claims a formula for calculating the stopping distance is:

$$D = \frac{x^2}{20} + x$$

where **D** is the **stopping distance** in **feet** and **x** is the **speed** in **mph**.
Compare the distances from the **formula** with those shown on the **data sheet**.

Three-second rule		Safe interval should be >	3 seconds	6 seconds
Speed	Distance travelled	For these conditions >	Good	Poor
25 mph	37 ft per second		111 ft	222 ft
35 mph	52 ft per second		166 ft	312 ft
45 mph	66 ft per second		198 ft	396 ft
55 mph	81 ft per second		243 ft	486 ft
65 mph	96 ft per second		288 ft	576 ft
75 mph	75 ft per second		333 ft	666 ft
			Safe following distance (feet)	

Task 3

Look at the **emergency braking graphs** on the data sheet. The first shows the **number of feet** travelled under **emergency braking** for speeds from **60 mph** and the **probability of a fatality**. This means that in a crash at **60 mph** there is a **50%** chance that the person involved will **die**. The second shows the **time** it takes to **brake from 60 mph** and the **probability of a fatality**.

These questions relate to **time** and **distance** after **emergency braking** from **60 mph**.

1 How **far** has a car travelled **before** the speed has **reduced** to **20 mph**?

2 How **long** does it take for the **speed** to **reduce** to **20 mph**?

3 **a** At what **speed** does the **chance** of a **fatality** become almost **zero**?
   b How **far** has the car **travelled** when it **reaches this speed**?
   c How **long** does it take to **reach this speed**?

4 How **long after braking** does the **chance** of a **fatality** reduce to **0.25**?

5 What is the **speed** after **1.5 seconds**?

6 How **far** has the car travelled during this **1.5 seconds**?

7 How **long** does it take the car to travel **20 feet**?

8 How **far** does the car travel in **1 second**?

9 What is the **speed** when the **chance** of a **fatality** is reduced to **1 in 10**?

10 Complete the graph for **time** against **stopping distance** for **emergency braking** from **60 mph**. Two points have already been plotted.

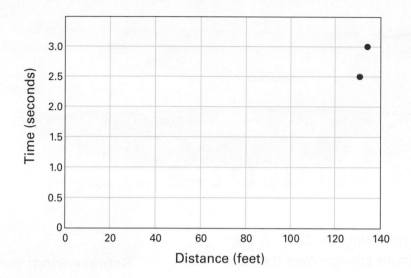

Emergency braking from 60 mph

Task 4 (extension)

Write a **letter** to the prime minister saying why you think the **speed limit** outside schools during school hours should be reduced to **20 mph**.

Climate change

These graphs show levels of carbon dioxide (CO_2) in the atmosphere and global temperature change over the last 150 years.

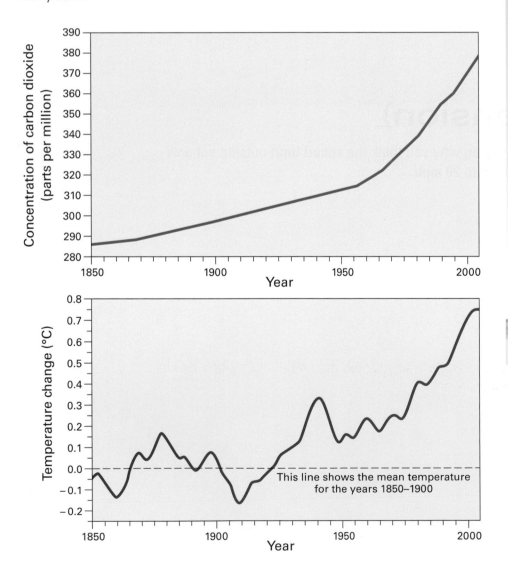

This line shows the mean temperature for the years 1850–1900

Learning objectives

Representing: decide how to represent the problem to make it easier to solve using mathematics

Analysing: use appropriate mathematical procedures

Interpreting: test generalisations and draw conclusions from the mathematical analysis

Performing: check work and methods when tackling a problem and decide if a different approach may be more effective

Links with
ICT, Science, Geography

These graphs show levels of carbon dioxide (CO_2) in the atmosphere and global temperature change over the last 400 000 years.

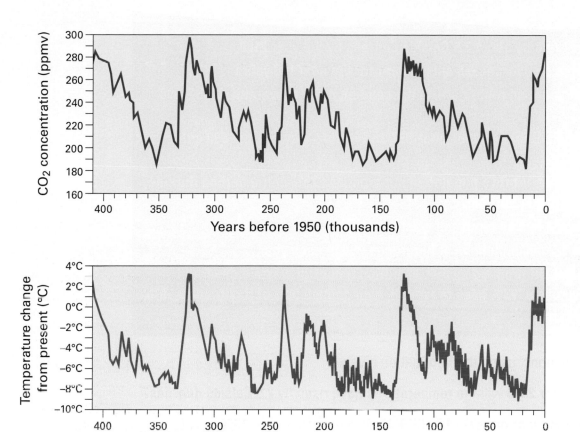

Task 1

Use both pairs of graphs to show that there is a link between the amount of carbon dioxide in the atmosphere and the global temperature.

Task 2

Here are some predictions and facts about global warming.

- **Temperatures will rise** by about **2.5 Celsius degrees** by the year **2100**.
- **Sea levels will rise** on average **0.5 cm per year** for the **next 100 years**.
- The **five warmest years** on record are, in **descending order of warmth**, 2005, 1998, 2002, 2003, 2004.
- **Glaciers are melting.** Between 1961 and 1997, the world's glaciers lost **890 cubic miles** of ice.
- The **USA** has **4%** of the **world's population** but produces **25%** of the **carbon dioxide pollution** from **fossil-fuel burning**.
- The **UK** produces 434 million tonnes of waste each year.
- The **UK** produces 5.2 million tonnes of hazardous waste each year.
- Householders in the **UK** produce almost **30 million tonnes** of waste on average **each year**. Of this waste, **73% goes to landfill**, even though **90% of it is recoverable** and could be **recycled**.

Answer the following questions, using the information given.

1   How many years **after 2010** will the temperatures have risen by 2.5 Celsius degrees?

2   The **second warmest** year on record is **1998**. How many years after 1998 was it before this **record was broken**?

3   The **UK** produces **434 million tonnes of waste** each year. Write **434 million** in figures.

4   By how many **metres** will **sea levels rise** in the **next 100 years**?

5   The **world population** is approximately **6800 million**. Use this to estimate the **population of the USA**. Give your answer to the **nearest 100 million**.

6   How many **tonnes** of **UK householders' waste** go to **landfill**?

7   What **fraction** of **UK householders' waste** that goes to landfill is **recoverable** and could be **recycled**?

8   There are about **9 million cubic miles** of ice on Earth. What **percentage** of this was lost **between 1961 and 1997**?

Task 3

Use the **graphs** to support the argument that **global warming is not happening**.

Use **other information** to support the argument that **global warming is caused by human behaviour**.

Growing, growing, grown...

This activity is about how some mathematical series grow very quickly. This is known as exponential growth.

Before you start, find a piece of scrap paper. It is said that, no matter how thin the paper may be, it is impossible to fold it more than seven times. Try it and see. If you have a tissue, try it with that. Did you manage more than seven folds?

The reason it gets so difficult to fold is that the number of layers you are folding doubles every time. When you start you have one layer. This is folded in half to give two layers. These are then folded to give four layers and so on. The number of layers each time is given by:

Fold	0	1	2	3	4	5	6	7	8	...
Layers after fold	1	2	4	8	16	32	64	128	256	...

So as you make the seventh fold you are trying to fold 64 layers. Imagine trying to fold 64 pieces of A4 paper in half! It can't be done.

Now think about this problem, which is very similar to the folding activity.

You have a piece of thin paper that is infinitely big. You cut it in half and place the two sheets together. You then cut these two sheets in half and place them together to give four sheets. You keep on doing this until you have made 50 cuts. How high will the resulting pile of paper be? Your teacher will tell you the answer later.

You will have met some simple powers such as square and cube. Powers are used to write long, repetitive multiplication calculations in a shortened way.

For example, $5 \times 5 \times 5 \times 5 \times 5 \times 5 \times 5 \times 5 \times 5$ can be written as 5^9

and 6^4 means $6 \times 6 \times 6 \times 6$.

The series for the number of sheets above can be written as:

$$2^0 \quad 2^1 \quad 2^2 \quad 2^3 \quad 2^4 \quad 2^5 \quad 2^6$$

and so on. Note that in mathematics anything raised to the power 0 is always 1 and anything raised to the power 1 is the same as itself. So:

$$2^0 = 1, \ 2^1 = 2, \ 2^2 = 2 \times 2 = 4, \ 2^3 = 2 \times 2 \times 2 = 8$$

and so on.

Questions

1   Continue these power series up to 10 terms.

   a 3^0 3^1 3^2 3^3 3^4 …   …   …   …   …

          1   3   9   …   …   …   …   …   …   …

   b 5^0 5^1 5^2 5^3 5^4 …   …   …   …   …

          1   5   25   …   …   …   …   …   …   …

   c 3×2^0 3×2^1 3×2^2 3×2^3 3×2^4 …   …   …   …   …

          3   6   12   …   …   …   …   …   …   …

2   Complete the following table, which shows the numerical value of powers of 10.

Number	0.0001		0.01	0.1	1		100			
Fraction			$\frac{1}{100}$	$\frac{1}{10}$	1	$\frac{10}{1}$				
Power		10^{-3}		10^{-1}	10^0	10^1	10^2	10^3	10^4	

3   **64 balls** are dropped into the **maze** shown in the diagram.
   At each point marked with a letter **half the balls** go to the left and **half** go to the **right**.
   So, at A, **32 balls** go to the **left** and **32** go to the **right**.
   At B, **16 balls** go to the **left** and **16** go to the **right**.
   Each ball lands in one of **five trays** at the bottom of the maze.

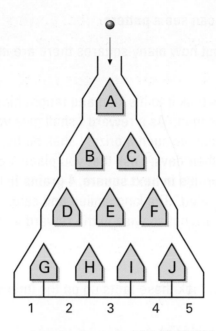

a Explain why **16** balls end up in **tray 2**. You may find it easier to copy the picture and mark how the 64 balls **split up** as they go through the maze.

b Work out how many balls end up in **each** of the **other trays**.

4 Imagine an alien from outer space arrives in Britain with a happiness bug on **1 January**. The number of people infected **doubles** each day. So on 2 January **four** people are infected, on 3 January **eight** people are infected and so on.

The population of Britain is approximately **61 million** people.

a On approximately what day of the year is the **whole population** infected? **Hint**: Use trial and improvement.

b Another alien also lands on **1 January** and spreads a love bug in the same way. The world has a population of **6800 million**. Will the **whole world** be in love before Valentine's Day (**14 February**)?

5 How many **squares** are there on a **chessboard**?

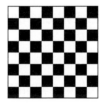

The answer is not 64.

Start by counting **how many squares** there are in one **small square**. □

Silly question, the answer is **one**.

Now count how many squares there are in a **2 x 2** board.

Not such a silly question, there are **five squares**:
four small 1 x 1 squares and one larger 2 x 2 square.

Now explain why there are **14 squares** in a **3 x 3 board**.

Count how many squares there are in a **4 x 4 board** and then a **5 x 5 board**.

Put your results in a **table** and see if you can see a **pattern**.

Once you see the pattern you can work out how many squares there are in an **8 x 8 board**.

6 The man who invented the game of **chess** took it to his king and taught him the game. The king was very pleased and said to the man: 'As a reward I shall give you your **weight in gold**.' The man said: 'I do not deserve such a prize, I shall be happy to have enough food to last my family the rest of their days. I ask that you place **1 grain of rice in first square** of the chessboard, **2 grains in next square**, **4 grains in the next square** and **so on until the 64th square** is filled.' The king smiled and said: 'You are wise enough to invent that game but you are not so wise in the reward you demand. Your wish is granted.'

Who got the **better deal**?

You will need the following information (or look these facts up on the internet to get the current values).

- One **kilogram** of **rice** contains **60 000 grains** of rice.
- A **tonne** is 1000 **kilograms**.
- A **tonne** of **rice** costs **£700**.
- Gold is worth **£22** a **gram**.
- The **average** weight of a man is **80 kg**.

Task 1 (extension)

Investigate the **Fibonacci** series:

1, 1, 2, 3, 5, 8, 13, 21, 34, …

- How many **terms** will there be **before 1000** is reached?
- What happens when you keep on **dividing consecutive pairs** of numbers:

    1 ÷ 1 = 1, 2 ÷ 1 = 2, 3 ÷ 2 = 1.5, 4 ÷ 3 = 1.33

and so on? What number do you eventually **end up with**?

- Where does the Fibonacci series occur in **nature**?

Recipes

Yorkshire pudding is a traditional accompaniment for roast beef. There are at least two different ways of preparing it.

The table below shows the guideline daily amounts (GDAs) of foods for women, men and children aged 5–10 years.

	Women	Men	Children 5–10 years
Energy (**kcalories**)	2000	2500	2000
Fat (g)	70	95	70
Of which saturated fat (g)	20	30	20
Carbohydrate (g)	230	300	220
Of which total **sugars** (g)	90	120	85
Non-milk extrinsic **sugars** (NMES) (g)	50	65	50
Protein (g)	45	55	24
Dietary fibre (AOAC) (g)	24	24	15
Dietary fibre (non-starch polysaccharide – NSP) (g)	18	18	11
Sodium (g)	2.4	2.4	1.4
Salt (g)	6	6	4

Here are two recipes for Yorkshire pudding, with additional information.

Recipe 1 – serves 8	Recipe 2 – serves 6
Ingredients	**Ingredients**
125 g plain flour	2 eggs
235 ml whole milk	235 ml milk
2 eggs	125 g plain flour
3 g salt	6 g salt
45 ml beef dripping or lard	240 g beef dripping or lard
Instructions	**Instructions**
1 In a large bowl, mix together the flour, milk, eggs and salt. Using an electric mixer, beat for 5 minutes, until the mixture is smooth. Cover and refrigerate for 1 hour.	1 Preheat the oven to 450 °F (230 °C). Put about a tablespoon of beef dripping into each pan of a 6-hole bun tin and place in the oven.
2 Preheat the oven to 425 °F (220 °C). Coat the base of a 9 × 13 inch baking tin with beef dripping. Heat the pan in the hot oven for 15 minutes so the dripping is hot and sizzling.	2 In a medium bowl, whisk the eggs until they are well blended. Stir in the milk, flour and salt. Pour mixture into the bun-tin so that each pan is about half-full.
3 Remove the mixture from the refrigerator. Beat it again by hand for about 30 seconds, then pour it into the baking tin. Bake for 20 minutes.	3 Bake for 15 minutes in the preheated oven, then reduce the oven temperature to 350 °F (180 °C) and bake for a further 15 minutes.
4 Lower the oven temperature to 375 °F (190 °C). Without opening the oven, continue baking for a further 15 minutes. The pudding should be puffed and golden brown. Remove from oven and serve hot.	
Amount per serving (Nutrition)	**Amount per serving (Nutrition)**
Calories (kcal): 106	Calories (kcal): 474
Total fat: 2.7 g	Total fat: 41.8 g
Cholesterol: 64 mg	Cholesterol: 114 mg
Sodium: 179 mg	Sodium: 646 mg
Total carbohydrate: 13.5 g	Total carbohydrate: 18.1 g
Dietary fibre: 0.4 g	Dietary fibre: 0.6 g
Protein: 6.4 g	Protein: 5.6 g

Task

You are preparing a dinner for **12 people**. Compare the two **recipes**, the **cooking instructions**, the **costs of ingredients** and the **guideline daily amounts**.

Decide which **recipe** to use to serve Yorkshire puddings.

Write a **report** that **justifies** your decisions. Include in your report any **advantages** or **disadvantages** of using each recipe.

Cost of Yorkshire pudding ingredients	
Free range eggs	£1.36 for 6
Milk	£1.65 for 2 litres
Flour	£1.30 for 1.5 kg
Salt	43p for 70 grams
Beef dripping (lard)	70p for 100 grams

Venting gas appliances

For this activity you will need the Data sheet: Venting gas appliances.

Gas appliances must have adequate venting systems to dispose of the waste gases, including carbon monoxide (CO), safely into the atmosphere. When gas appliances do not have adequate venting systems, people can die of carbon monoxide poisoning.

Governments set down minimum standards for venting systems. These must be followed by builders and gas fitters so that gas appliances are safe.

Data sheet: Venting gas appliances shows the minimum requirements for a gas vent pipe that emerges through a roof. It also gives a table of data for the maximum permitted output in thousands of British thermal units (Btus) per hour.

> A **British thermal unit** (Btu) is a measure of **energy**.
>
> **Inches** are abbreviated as, for example, **9"**.
>
> **Feet** are abbreviated as, for example, **6'**.

Look at the first page of the Data sheet: Venting gas appliances. The diagram shows a typical configuration for a gas vent pipe emerging from a roof.

It must be at least 8 feet from a vertical wall.

The pitch of a roof is a measure of the steepness. It is calculated by measuring how many inches a roof rises vertically for every 12 inches horizontally.

Task 1

Refer to the Data sheet: Venting gas appliances. Use the table showing the **roof pitch and minimum height of vent** to answer these questions.

1   What is the **pitch** for a flat roof?

2   What is the **minimum height** for a roof with a pitch of **10.5/12**?

3   What is the **maximum pitch** possible for a pipe of **height 7 feet**?

4   A roof has a **vertical rise of 3 feet for every 4 feet horizontally**. What is the minimum height of a vent pipe for this roof?

5   Copy and complete this step graph.

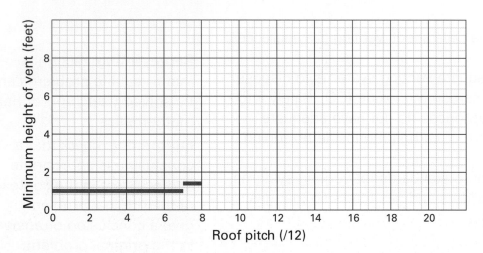

Task 2

The diagrams below are **drawn to scale**. Each square represents an area of **1 foot by 1 foot**.

Decide if the following vent pipes meet the **minimum requirements**.

If they do not, explain why.

a
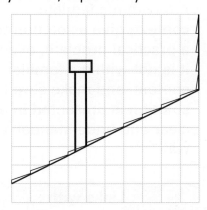

b
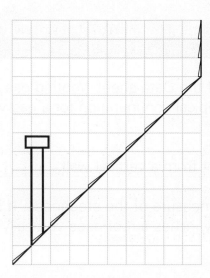

Task 3

Copy these diagrams and draw a vent of the **appropriate height** and in an **acceptable position** for each of these roofs.

a

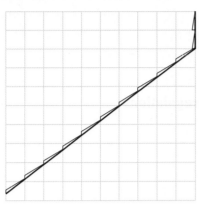

b

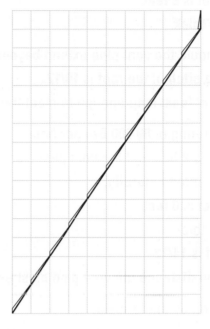

> Look at the second page of the data sheet. The table shows the **maximum allowable output** of a **single gas appliance** for **different vent arrangements**.
>
> For example, a vent pipe with a **diameter of 6 inches**, a **lateral distance of 5 feet** and a **height of 10 feet** could have a minimum of **52 000 Btu per hour** and a maximum of **280 000 for a fan-assisted system** and **188 000 for a naturally ventilated system**.

Task 4

1   An appliance has an output of **200 000 Btu per hour**.

   It is fitted in a room where there is **no room for a lateral pipe** so the vent pipe rises **vertically**.

   The vent pipe is **4 inches** in diameter and there will be a fan fitted.

   What is the **minimum height** of the pipe?

2   A gas fitter measures for an installation. She works out that the **lateral distance possible** is **5 feet** and the **minimum height** for the vertical pipe is **15 feet**.

   She intends to fit a fan to the vent pipe.

   What is the **minimum diameter** of pipe, if the householder wants an appliance that produces **at least 250 000 Btu per hour**?

3 An appliance has a rating of **300 000 Btu per hour**.

   The lateral distance is **5 feet** and the vent pipe diameter is **7 inches**.

   The system will be vented **naturally**.

   The height to the roof is **8 feet**.

   The roof is **6 inches** thick.

   a By how much should the vent pipe extend **beyond the roof**?

   b Now assume the **pitch** of the roof is **10/12**.

   Will the pipe be **at least** long enough to meet the **minimum height regulations**?

4 An appliance has a rating of **80 000 Btu per hour**.

   The lateral distance is **2 feet** and the vent pipe diameter is **4 inches**.

   The system will be vented **naturally**.

   The height to the roof is **6 feet**.

   The roof is **6 inches** thick.

   The pitch of the roof is **14/12**.

   What is the **minimum distance** the vent pipe must extend **beyond the roof**?

5 The **flow area** is given by the formula:

$$\text{flow area} = \pi \left(\frac{D}{4}\right)^2 \text{ square inches}$$

   Calculate the **flow area** for pipes of the following **diameters**. Give your answer to the **nearest whole number**.

   a 3 inches   b 5 inches   c 8 inches   d 9 inches

Task 5 (extension)

In the diagrams for this task, **each square** represents an area of **2 feet by 2 feet**.

1 What are the **minimum, maximum with a fan** and **maximum with natural ventilation** in **thousands of Btu per hour** for these vent systems?

a

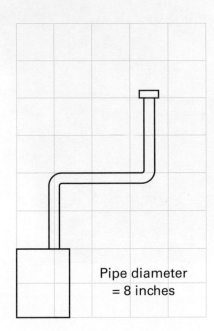

Pipe diameter
= 8 inches

b

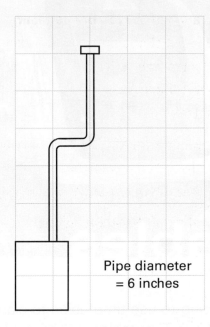

Pipe diameter
= 6 inches

2 The diagram shows an appliance with a rating of **100 000 Btu per hour**. Design a vent system for the appliance. Use a vent pipe with a diameter of **6 inches**, venting from the appliance **vertically** into the **loft space**, as shown. Complete the diagram so that the venting system **meets all the necessary regulations**. The system will be **naturally ventilated**.

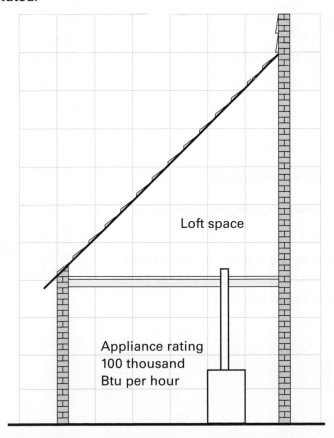

Loft space

Appliance rating
100 thousand
Btu per hour

Timetables

In this activity, you are going to use timetables to plan a journey. You will need the Data sheet: Timetables, or you could use internet searches.

Task

Suppose you live in **Trefforest** and want to visit **Brussels**. You want to spend **two nights** there and you decide to travel by **Eurostar**.

You decide to go on a **Saturday** and return on a **Monday**.

Your **outward journey** is:

- by train from Trefforest to Cardiff Central
- by train from Cardiff Central to London Paddington
- by Eurostar from London St Pancras to Brussels.

Plan the **journey to Brussels** and the **return journey**.

Allow **at least 15 minutes** between trains at **Cardiff Central**.

You have to **check in for Eurostar** at least **30 minutes before departure**.

Allow **20 minutes** for the **journey from London Paddington to London St Pancras**.

The **times of arrival and departure in Brussels** are given as **local times** and are **1 hour ahead** of UK times. This means you need to **add on 1 hour** to the London time to find the **equivalent time** in Brussels.

Learning objectives

Representing: recognise that a real-life problem can be solved using appropriate mathematics

Analysing: find a result or solution to the original problem

Interpreting: give a conclusion or answer to the original problem, using language and forms of presentation that make sense to a wider population

Performing: analyse the situation or problem and decide which is the appropriate mathematical method needed to tackle it

Links with
ICT, French, Geography

You could use a table like this to help you plan the trip.

	Time	Time taken
Depart Trefforest		–
Arrive Cardiff Central		
Depart Cardiff Central		
Arrive London Paddington		
Depart London Paddington		
Arrive London St Pancras		
Depart London St Pancras		
Arrive Brussels		
		Total time taken =

	Time	Time taken
Depart Brussels		–
Arrive London St Pancras		
Depart London St Pancras		
Arrive London Paddington		
Depart London Paddington		
Arrive Cardiff Central		
Depart Cardiff Central		
Arrive Trefforest		
		Total time taken =

Alcohol

Excessive consumption of alcohol is a growing problem in the United Kingdom (UK), especially among young people. It is common for young people to drink to excess, especially at weekends, in what is called binge drinking. In the UK, binge drinking is defined as consuming more than half of the weekly recommended alcohol intake in one session. It is estimated that 54% of 15–21-year-olds binge drink regularly.

This graph shows the average amount of alcohol consumed by people over 14 in the UK over the last century. The graph shows the amount of pure alcohol consumed.

Annual average alcohol consumption per person over 14 in the UK for 1900–2000

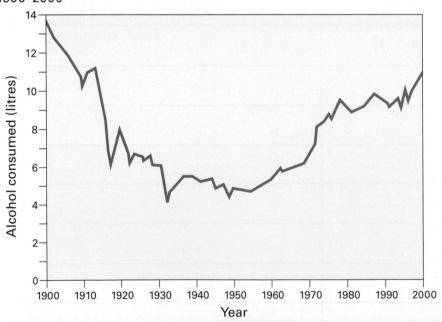

Learning objectives

Representing: recognise that a real-life problem can be solved using appropriate mathematics

Analysing: use appropriate mathematical procedures

Interpreting: interpret results and solutions and make a generalisation about them

Performing: give a solution to a practical problem, even if it is not within a familiar context, and make sure the solution is presented in a clear and understandable way; draw a conclusion from working and provide a mathematical justification for this conclusion

Links with
Art and History

1 pint ≈ 0.57 litres
1 litre ≈ 1.76 pints
1 litre = 10 dl = 100 cl = 1000 ml

1 pound (lb) ≈ 0.45 kg
1 kilogram (kg) ≈ 2.2 lbs

Task 1

1 Give reasons why the consumption of alcohol was **highest** in the early years of the last century.

2 Since approximately **what year** has the consumption been increasing steadily?

3 Estimate the **average consumption** of alcohol in 2010, if the trend continues.

4 A 333 ml bottle of German lager contains **5% alcohol by volume** (ABV). How many bottles will it take to provide **1 litre of alcohol**?

5 A 75 cl bottle of red wine contains **14% ABV**. How many bottles will it take to provide **1 litre of alcohol**?

Task 2

In the UK, a **unit of alcohol** is defined as **10 millilitres** (or approximately **8 grams**) of **ethanol** (**ethyl alcohol**).

The number of units of alcohol in a drink can be calculated by multiplying the **volume** of the drink (in **millilitres**, ml) by its **percentage ABV** and **dividing by 1000**. Thus, one pint (**568 ml**) of beer at **4% ABV** contains:

$$\frac{568 \times 4}{1000} = 2.3 \text{ units}$$

If the volume is given in **centilitres** then the formula reduces to the **volume** multiplied by the **ABV as a decimal**.

So **75 centilitres** of wine at **13% ABV** contains **75 × 0.13 = 9.75 units**

Since 1995 the UK Government has advised that:

- regular consumption of 3–4 units of alcohol a day for men and 2–3 units a day for women would not pose significant health risks
- consistently drinking four or more units a day (men) or three or more units a day (women) is not advisable.

1 How many units are there in each of the following drinks?

   a A **75 cl** bottle of sherry with **20% ABV**

   b A **litre** bottle of whisky with **40% ABV**

   c A **275 ml** bottle of an alcopop with **5% ABV**

   d A **pint** of mild beer with **2.8% ABV**

   e A **half-pint** of strong lager with **8% ABV**

2 What is the ABV of each of these drinks?

   a A **70 cl** bottle of cognac that contains **38 units**

   b A **litre** bottle of vodka that contains **37.5 units**

c A **75 cl** bottle of white wine that contains **8.25 units**

d A **180 ml** bottle of barley wine that contains **1.5 units**

e A **pint** of shandy that contains **1 unit**.

3 How many **333 ml** bottles of German lager with **5% ABV** could a **man** drink before passing the daily unit limit?

4 How many **12.5 cl** glasses of red wine with an **ABV of 14%** could a **woman** drink before passing the daily limit for women?

5 A **man** drinks **8 pints** of beer with **3.8% ABV** and **two 30 ml** shots of whisky with **40% ABV** on a Friday evening.

   a How many **units** of alcohol does he consume?

   b How many **centilitres** of alcohol does he consume?

Task 3

In the UK, and in most other countries, drink–driving is considered to be a serious offence. The limit for driving in the UK is **80 ml of alcohol per litre of blood** or **8% blood alcohol**. Alcohol inhibits reaction times and causes drivers to feel over-confident, which leads to many accidents.

Look at Data sheet: Alcohol. You will need to refer to it to answer these questions.

1 A **woman** weighing **140 lbs** drinks a **pint** of beer with **4% ABV**. Would she be **legally intoxicated**?

2 A **woman** drives to a restaurant in her car. She weighs **160 lbs**. During the meal, which takes **2 hours** she drinks two **125 ml** glasses of white wine with **11% ABV**. Is she safe to drive home?

3 Over the course of a Friday evening from **8 pm to 11 pm** a **man** weighing **160 lbs** drinks **4 pints** of beer with **3.8% ABV**. Work out his **probable blood alcohol percentage**.

4 Four teenagers – two girls and two boys – obtain a **2-litre** bottle of cheap cider with **7.5% ABV**. The girls weigh **100 lbs each** and the boys weigh **120 lbs each**. They share the cider equally. Work out the **probable blood alcohol percentage** of each of them.

5 Every Sunday lunchtime a man, weighing **160 lbs**, drives his family to a local pub for lunch. He drinks **1 pint** of beer with **3.5% ABV** and a **250 ml** glass of wine with **12% ABV**. The meal lasts **90 minutes**. After the meal the family go for a walk. How long should the walk last if he is to be **safe enough to drive home**?

Task 4 (extension)

Design a poster warning of the effects of drink–driving.

Garden designer

You have probably seen TV shows where people go to a house where the garden looks awful and, with some effort, change it into a something completely different.

Imagine that you work as a garden designer.

You have been sent to a new house to give an estimate for a job.

Here is a sketch of the garden area.

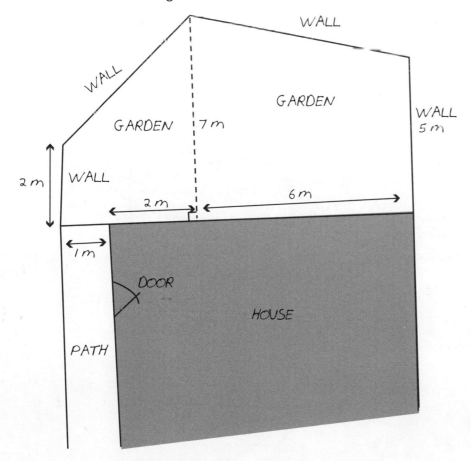

⭐⭐⭐⭐

Learning objectives

Representing: recognise that a real-life problem can be solved using appropriate mathematics; decide how to represent the problem to make it easier to solve using mathematics

Analysing: analyse a pattern or a relationship, using appropriate techniques

Interpreting: interpret results and solutions and make a generalisation about them; check that a conclusion is appropriate and accurate in the context of the original problem

Performing: use a range of mathematics to find solutions; check work and methods when tackling a problem and decide if a different approach may be more effective

Links with
ICT, Design and Technology

Task 1

Using **centimetre-squared paper** and a **scale of 1 cm to represent 1 metre**, make two accurate **scale drawings** of the garden shown in the sketch.

You will use these in **Task 2** and **Task 3**.

Task 2

The home-owner wants the garden design to include the **following features**.

There should be:

- a **path** along the **wall** of the house – you can choose how wide it is
- a **seating area** close to the house
- a **lawn** that has an **area of at least 16 m²**
- a **circular pond** of **radius 1 metre**
- a **flower bed** that is **half a metre wide** and **between 3 metres and 4 metres long**
- **two trees** that have to be **more than 2 metres from the house wall** and **at least 3 metres apart**
- a **rockery** next to one wall – its **area** has to be **between 2 m² and 5 m².**

Design the garden.

Include all the **measurements** on your diagram.

Task 3

Using exactly the **same rules as in Task 2**, redesign the garden to give the homeowner a **choice of designs**.

Saving energy

The effects of global warming and increasing costs of energy are likely to affect everyone. In this activity, a family is trying to work out how they can save money and reduce carbon emissions.

Your role is that of a consultant who can help the family take sensible decisions. This is your business card.

I. M. Green

Energy-saving consultant

Call me to save money on your energy bills

01234–555–6789
imgreen@alo.co.uk

Mr and Mrs Patel have asked you to give them advice about saving money, especially on their annual gas and electricity bills.

This is a plan of their bungalow. Each square represents 1 square metre.

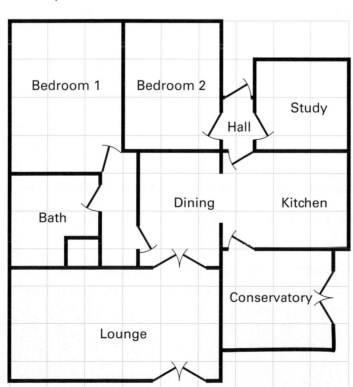

Learning objectives

Representing: decide how to represent the problem to make it easier to solve using mathematics

Interpreting: check that a conclusion is appropriate and accurate in the context of the original problem; give a conclusion or answer to the original problem, using language and forms of presentation that make sense to a wider population

Performing: give a solution to a practical problem, even if it is not within a familiar context, and make sure the solution is presented in a clear and understandable way; draw a conclusion from working and provide a mathematical justification for this conclusion

Links with
ICT, Geography, Science

Room area (m^2)	Minimum Btu (per hour)
6 ≤ area < 8	1800
8 ≤ area < 10	2100
10 ≤ area < 12	2400
12 ≤ area < 14	2700
14 ≤ area < 18	3000

This table shows the minimum radiator output required per hour, in British thermal units (Btu), for rooms of various areas.

Task 1

The Patel's have a radiator in each of their rooms **except the hall**.

Calculate an approximate value for the **minimum Btu (per hour)** they will need for each room.

They run their heating from 6 am to 8 am and from 4 pm to 10.30 pm on weekdays and from 6 am to 10.30 pm on Saturdays and Sundays. Calculate their **approximate annual Btu use**.

> One and a half million Btu ≈ 60 kg of carbon dioxide gas (CO_2)

How many tonnes of CO_2 does the Patels' heating system produce each year?

Task 2

The Patel's have a daughter called Zeenat.

Their **annual bills** are:
- **electricity £540**
- **gas £720**
- **water £640**.

Assume that their use of energy other than heating produces about **1 tonne of CO_2 per year**.

The diagram below shows the **cost**, **saving (£) per year** and **saving in CO_2 per year** of the various energy-saving methods.

Write a report for the Patels, outlining the **costs**, **savings** and **how long it would take** them to get their money back if they bought a new set of energy-saving appliances, for example. You **do not** have to **include** every energy-saving measure.

Action Annual	CO₂ saving	Annual cost saving
Turn down the heating by 1°C	330 kg	£40
Switch off electrical goods when not in use	153 kg	£40
Turn off the tap		£7 per tap
Dry clothes on the line	311 kg	£15
Draught proofing	150 kg	£25 (cost of DIY: £90)
Use shower instead of bath		£22 per person
Set hot water to 60°C	145 kg	£10
Use energy-saving bulbs	40 kg	£9 (cost: 49p each)
Use Savaplug on fridge	100 kg	Save £12 (cost: £25)
Fill kettle with only as much water as required	48 kg	
Replace old appliances with energy-efficient ones	85 kg	£70 (cost approx: £1000)
Double-glaze windows	720 kg	£110 (cost approx: £400 per room)
Fill up the dishwasher before using		Save £15
Insulate loft	1 tonne	£150 (cost of DIY: £250)
Install solar electric power	1.2 tonne	Half of the electricity bill (cost: £6000 to £15000)
Fit foil behind radiators	51 kg	(cost: £15)
Install wind power generator	250 kg	One-third of the electricity bill (cost: from £1500)
Insulate cavity walls	800 kg	£120 (cost: £500)

Ways to save energy and the planet – annual savings for each energy-savings measure

Task 3 (extension)

The Patels currently drive an old car that produces **160 g of CO₂ per kilometre**. They travel **16 000 km per year** by car. The car does about **7.5 kilometres to a litre** of fuel. Use the internet to research the **least polluting** cars. Advise the Patel's about whether it will be worth their while buying a newer model.

Rich Tasks

Rugby numbers

In a game of Rugby Union you score points as follows.

Try	5 points
Conversion	2 points
Drop goal	3 points
Penalty goal	3 points

You can only attempt a conversion after you have scored a try.
A converted try is worth 7 points (5 + 2).
An unconverted try is worth 5 points.

Here is the result of a rugby match played on 4 April 2009.

Leicester	37 points	5 tries 3 conversions 2 penalties
Sale	31 points	3 tries 2 conversions 4 penalties

Learning objectives

Representing: decide which methods to use to make progress with the solution

Analysing: establish a pattern or relationship and then change the variables to see how this changes the results; test generalisations and draw conclusions from the mathematical analysis

Performing: use mathematical skills and knowledge to make progress on a problem, even if it does not use a routine mathematical procedure; analyse the situation or problem and decide which is the appropriate mathematical method needed to tackle it

Links with
ICT and PE

Task 1

You may choose to work **in pairs** for this task.

Check that the **score** shown above is **correct**.

Can you find a **different way** in which **Sale** could have scored **31 points**?

Task 2

You may choose to work **in pairs** for this task.

Explain why it **impossible** for a team to score **exactly 4 points**.
What other **total numbers of points** are **impossible**?

Some totals can be reached in **more than one way**.
Explore the **different ways** in which **total scores** can be achieved.

> The way points are scored has changed over the years.
>
> **Until 1971** a **try** was worth **3 points**.
>
> From **1971 to 1992** a **try** was worth **4 points**.
>
> A **try** has been worth **5 points** since **1992**.

Task 3

You may choose to work **in pairs** for this task.

What would the **scores** in the **match above** have been if a **try** had been **worth 4 points** or **3 points**?
Would the **winner** have been **different** in **either case**?

Task 4

You may choose to work **in pairs** for this task.

Can you think of some results for which the **winner** using a **5-point-try** scoring system would **lose** using a **3-point-try** scoring system?
Can you **generalise** your findings?
Why do you think that the **number of points** for a **try** was **increased**?

Join a group

How often do you get to work in a group in a class?

Do you enjoy it or do you prefer to work alone?

If you have to work in a group, do you prefer big groups or small groups?

Which work best?

Learning objectives

Representing: recognise that a real-life problem can be solved using appropriate mathematics

Analysing: establish a pattern or relationship and then change the variables to see how this changes the results

Interpreting: test generalisations and draw conclusions from the mathematical analysis

Performing: use mathematical skills and knowledge to make progress on a real-life problem, even if the situation described is not within a familiar context; use a range of mathematics to find solutions

Task 1

How are students **grouped** in your class?
How many **pairs** could there be?
How many **threes**? And **fours**?

Think of how the class is grouped in **another subject**.
Are the group sizes **different**? Describe the **differences**.

Task 2

There are **30 students** in a class.
A teacher wants to divide them into **groups**.
All the groups must be the **same size**.
No one should be **left out**.

Suggest how the teacher could do it.

Task 3

Work in **pairs**.

Make a sketch of your classroom.

Show how it could be arranged so that **30 students** could work in **groups of equal size**.

Is it a **good arrangement**?

What should you think about if you want to answer this?

Task 4

Make an accurate **scale drawing** of your classroom.

Now show on your drawing the **best way** to arrange the classroom for **30 students** to work in **groups**.

All groups must be the **same size**.

You can **choose the group size**.

Evaluate your arrangement.

Task 5

Not all classes have 30 students.

Investigate what group sizes are possible for **classes of different sizes**.
Remember all **group sizes** should be the **same**.
Choose **sensible class sizes** to investigate.
Are there any class sizes that **don't work**?

Task 6 (extension)

There are **two classes** working together in the hall.
There are about **60 students**.
Investigate possible **group sizes**.

Follow that car

Cars have number plates so that they can be identified uniquely.

The registration letters on a car show where it was first registered.

Do cars tend to stay where they were registered or do they move around the country?

In this activity you will investigate what information you can find out about a car just from its number plate.

You will need the Data sheet: Follow that car.

Task 1

Think of a car that you know that was registered **after 1 September 2001**.
Find out all you can from its **number plate**.
You could use the internet to help you.

Task 2

Think up one or two questions you could ask someone about **car registration codes** to see if that person understands how to **decode** them.

Task 3

Investigate cars **in your area** that have **new-style number plates**.

What **hypotheses** could you test?

What **questions** could you ask?

Choose a topic about car registration to **investigate**.

Write a **brief plan**, including the **data** you need to collect and what you will do with it.

Task 4

Carry out your **enquiry** from Task 3.

Present your results in any way that you think is suitable.

Bike race

Bicycle track racing is a sport in which Britain does well. It requires very high levels of fitness and great dedication in training.

You will need the Data sheet: Bike race for this activity.

Task 1

Study the result of the **one-kilometre time trial** in the **World Cycling Championships**.

Who **won**? What was his **winning time**?

Write down five interesting facts from the data.

Task 2

Look at the details of the **medal winners**.

These are the riders who came **first, second** and **third**.

Analyse their performances and, in particular, compare their **times** and **positions** as the **race progressed**.

Draw up appropriate **graphs** and **charts** to do this.

Think carefully about the **best type of graph or chart** to use.

Include a **brief description** of any **interesting features**.

Learning objectives

Representing: decide how to represent the problem to make it easier to solve using mathematics

Analysing: use appropriate mathematical procedures

Interpreting: give a conclusion or answer to the original problem, using language and forms of presentation that make sense to a wider population

Performing: use mathematical skills and knowledge to make progress on a real-life problem, even if the situation described is not within a familiar context; analyse the situation or problem and decide which is the appropriate mathematical method needed to tackle it

Links with
PE

Task 3

From the data you have been given, you could work out the time for a rider to travel **each 125 metres** of the race. How do you think these will vary?

Do some **calculations** to see if you are correct.

It may be **different** for different riders.

You could show your times on a **chart or graph**.

Task 4

Is it possible to work out the **exact speed** of a rider at any time?

Use **average speeds** to **estimate** the **fastest speeds** of some riders.

How much difference is there between the **fastest** and the **slowest** riders?

Useful information

$$\text{Average speed} = \frac{\text{distance travelled}}{\text{time taken}}$$

1 km/h = 0.62 mph

1 m/s = 2.24 mph

In 2007 the **world record** distance **cycled in one hour** from a **standing start** was set by **Ondrej Sosenka**. He travelled **49.700 km** (30.88 miles).

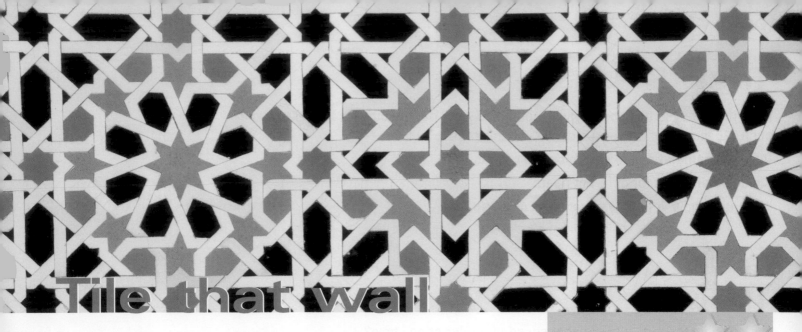

Tile that wall

Wall tiles are usually placed according to a pattern that looks attractive.

One of the ways of creating a pleasing pattern is to use symmetry.

Task 1

Suppose you have four tiles like this:

Can you arrange them to make a **symmetrical image**?

Can you do it in **different ways**?

Think about **reflection symmetry** or **rotation symmetry** or **translations**…

Links with Art and Design

Task 2

Work in pairs for this task.

Imagine you are a designer for a company that makes tiles.

Your brief is to **design a square tile** that can make an interesting **symmetrical pattern** to cover a wall.

There are some restrictions which will help keep down the cost.

- Your design should be **simple to draw**.
- You can only use **white** and **one other colour**.

Design a suitable tile.

Show how your tile can be used to make an **interesting symmetrical pattern**.

Be prepared to **describe the symmetries** in your pattern.

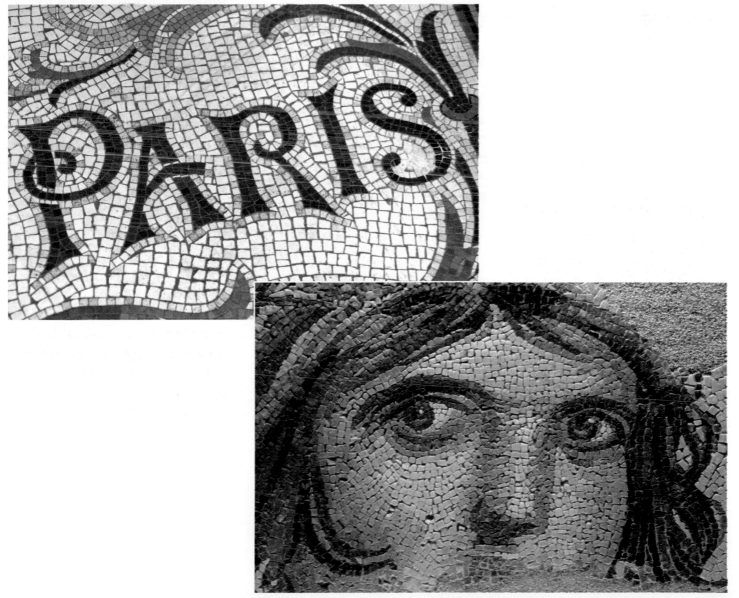

Body mass index

The body mass index (BMI) is a measure used to show if an adult is at a healthy weight.

Here is a formula for calculating BMI.

$$\text{BMI} = (\text{weight in kg}) \div (\text{height in m})^2$$

A person with BMI between 18.5 and 25 is at a healthy weight.
A person with BMI less that 18.5 is underweight.
A person with BMI between 25 and 30 is overweight.
A person with BMI over 30 is obese.

This does not apply to children. A different method is used for them.

Task 1

Look at these four people.

Here are the **heights** and **weights** of four people,
A, B, C and D, but not in any particular order.

| **Height** (m) | 1.75 | 1.20 | 1.65 | 1.60 |
| **Weight** (kg) | 53 | 31 | 57 | 80 |

Decide whether each of them is **underweight**, **healthy**, **overweight** or **obese**.

Task 2

A woman is **1.63 m tall** and **weighs 43.5 kg**.

She is worried that she is **overweight**. What advice can you give her?

Task 3

Work in **pairs**.

A man with a **BMI of 25** is on the **borderline** of being **overweight**. Work out some **possible heights** and **weights** for him.

Task 4

Work in groups of **four**.

Produce a **poster** that **adults** can use to decide whether they are at a **healthy weight**.

> Some people only know their **height** in **feet** and **inches** and their **weight** in **stones** and **pounds**.
>
> 1 foot = 30.5 cm or 0.305 m   12 inches = 1 foot
>
> 1 inch = 2.54 cm
>
> 1 stone = 6.35 kg   14 pounds = 1 stone
>
> 1 pound = 0.454 kg

Task 5 (extension)

My dad is **6 feet tall** and **weighs 15 stone**.

He says his **BMI** = $15 \div 6^2 = 15 \div 36 = 0.417$.

That can't be right! What has gone wrong? What is the correct answer?

Task 6 (extension)

Phil Vickery is a rugby player. He was in the England team that won the Rugby World Cup in 2003.

When he played for England he was **1.90 m tall** and **weighed 125 kg**.

Do you think he was overweight?

Green travel

Carbon dioxide is one of the greenhouse gases that contribute to global warming.

The Government has put cars into seven bands, based on their carbon dioxide emissions.

Band	Carbon dioxide (CO$_2$) emissions (g/km)
A	0–100
B	101–120
C	121–150
D	151–165
E	166–185
F	186–225
G	Over 225

For example, a Range Rover gives out about 300 g/km and a Ford Fiesta gives about 150 g/km, depending on the model.
Cars with higher emissions pay more road tax. Cars in band A pay none.

You can find ready reckoners to give information about cars' carbon dioxide emissions and the tax bands on the internet.

Figures for other types of transport can also be found on the internet or the Data sheet: Green travel.

Links with Science

Task 1

Explain what **g/km** means.

What do you think the **CO₂ emission rate** is for any cars in your family?

If your family does not have a car, think about a car belonging to someone you know.

Task 2

Suppose you came to school **by car** every day.

How much **carbon dioxide** would the car **emit** into the atmosphere **in a year**, carrying you **to and from school**?

Task 3

Suppose you work as a **green travel consultant**.

A client who **travels regularly** to various parts of **Great Britain** has asked for your advice about the **CO₂ emissions** for the different ways she travels.

She could travel by **car**, **train**, **coach** or **plane**.

Your task is to give her some **comparative figures** for **CO₂ emissions**, for travelling from **London to Edinburgh**.

Then find similar figures for **typical journeys** in your **local area**.

The distance from **London to Edinburgh**, by road, is **661 km**.

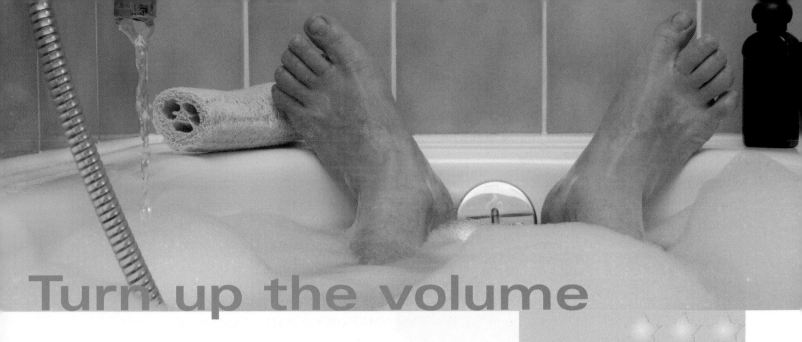

Turn up the volume

Volume is a measure of how big an object is. It is easy to measure the volume of boxes but in this activity you will find out how to measure the volume of irregular shapes such as people.

Task 1

How can you find the **volume** of a **cereal box**?

What **units** will you use for the answer?

How **accurately** can you give the answer?

Task 2

Do this activity in pairs.

Can you find the **volume** of a **person**?

What **methods** can you think of for doing this?

Your task is to choose a method and estimate the volume of a person as accurately as you can.

You should be able to explain your method to someone else.

Task 3 (extension)

In 1946 Robert Earl Hughes was the **world's fattest man** and he still holds the world record for the largest **chest measurement: 10 feet 4 inches**.

Source: *Guinness Book of Records*

When he died he was buried in a **coffin** the size of a **piano case**.

Can you estimate the volume of Robert Earl Hughes and compare it to the volume of a 'normal' pupil?

Useful information:

1 foot is approximately 30 cm

1 inch is approximately 2.5 cm

Task 4 (extension)

Can you estimate the **volume** of a **baby**?

How did you do it?

Give us a job

Getting a job can seem like the answer to all your problems. You have money to spend and things to spend it on. The reality is often tougher than people expect.

Task 1

Look at the **job description** and **salary** on the card you are given. Imagine you have **just started** this job.

How much will you be **earning per week**?

How would you like to **spend this money**?

Task 2

You will have to pay **income tax** and **national insurance** in your new job.

How much will you have to pay?

Will you have to **adjust** your **spending plans**?

Task 3

You have decided to live **away from home**.

You want to **share a house** or a **flat** with some friends.

Do some **research** to find out how much this will **cost** you.

How much money have you **got left** now?

How will you **spend it**?

Task 4

Have you included **food** in your **spending plans**?

Estimate how much you will spend **in a week** on **food**.

How much have you got **left** now?

Task 5

What **other things** will you have to pay for?

Try to make an **estimate** of those costs.

Have you got **any money left**?

Task 6 (extension)

Many people like to have a **car**.

Your granddad has offered to **give you his car** because he cannot drive any more.

Can you **afford** to **run it** on your **salary**?

Populations

Is the size of a country is directly related to the number of people who live there? In this activity, you will investigate.

There are many websites where you can find out about the populations and the areas of the countries of the world.

> The **population density** of a country is calculated as
>
> $$\text{population density} = \frac{\text{population}}{\text{area}}$$
>
> For example, in the **2001 census** the **population** of England was **49 181 000 people** and the **area** was **130 281 km²**.

Learning objectives

Representing: decide how to represent the problem to make it easier to solve using mathematics

Analysing: use appropriate mathematical procedures

Interpreting: interpret results and solutions and make a generalisation about them

Performing: analyse the situation or problem and decide which is the appropriate mathematical method needed to tackle it; check work and methods when tackling a problem and decide if a different approach may be more effective

Links with
ICT and Geography

Task 1

1   Check that the **population density** of **England** in **2001** was **377 people per km²**.

2   The **population density** of **Scotland** is **66 people per km²**.

Based on the two population densities, which of these statements must be true?

   A England has a bigger population than Scotland.

   B England has a bigger area than Scotland.

   C English cities are bigger than Scottish cities.

   D England is more crowded than Scotland.

   E England is a nicer place to live than Scotland.

3   A friend asks you to explain what the **population density** tells you **about a country**. What will you say?

Task 2

Work in pairs for this task if you wish.

Refer to Data sheet: Populations, which shows the **populations** and the **areas** of all the countries of the world. Think of some **questions** you could ask. Here are some examples.

- Do the **largest countries** have the **biggest populations**?

- Which countries in **Europe** have **similar population densities** to that of the **UK**?

- How much do the populations of **African** countries vary?

- Think of some **more questions** you could answer, using the **Data sheet**.

- How could you **change** each question into a **hypothesis to test**?

Task 3 (investigation)

Choose a **question or hypothesis** from Task 2.

Use the **Data sheet** to find the information you will need to **answer your question** or **test your hypothesis**.

Carry out the **investigation** and write down your **conclusion**. Include **evidence** such as **charts** or **graphs** to support your conclusion.

Be prepared to **present your findings** in a **discussion** with the rest of the class.

With thanks to Frome Community College.

The publishers wish to thank the following for permission to reproduce photographs:

Cover image © Bob Battersby, BDI Images

Pages 8, 10, 11, 13, 14, 16, 20, 23, 26, 28, 29, 32, 34, 35, 38, 39, 40, 43, 46, 49, 50, 54, 57, 59, 64, 68, 69, 71, 74, 78, 81, 84, 85, 87, 92, 94, 95, 96, 97, 98, 99, 104, 105, 106, 107t, 107b 108, 109, 110, 112, 113t, 113b, 114, 117, 118, 119, 120, 121, 122, 123, 124 © istockphoto.com
Page 60 © photos.com
Map on page 22 © Collins Bartholomew Ltd 2009

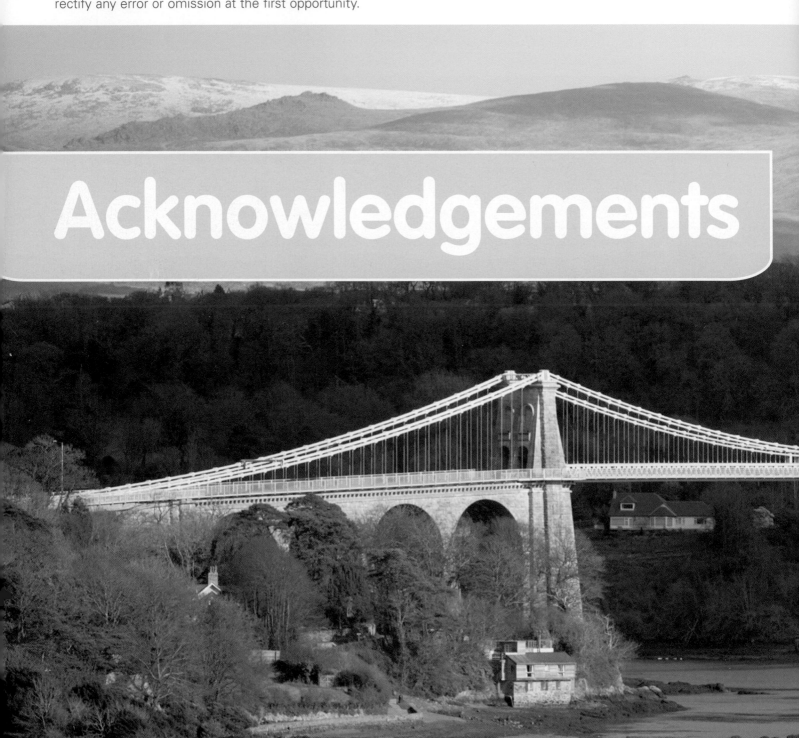

Acknowledgements

The End